Backpackers Poetry: An Anthology of Poems Selected for the Backpacker and Adventure Traveler

Edited By

David Thibault

Lunar Press, LLC

Tucson

Lunar Press, LLC
Publisher since 2010
7879 N Rockwood Place
Tucson, AZ 85741
www.LunarPress.com

ISBN: 978-0-9833986-0-8

Printed in the United States of America

ACKNOWLEDGEMENTS

Special thanks are given for the privilege of reprinting poems in this book:

James Wright, "Lying in a Hammock at William Duffy's Farm in Pine Island, Minnesota" from Collected Poems ©1971 by James Wright, and reprinted with permission of Wesleyan University Press.

"Firewarden on Kerrsage,", "Altitude," and "Eagle Plain" Reprinted from *Robert Francis Collected Poems 1936-1976*. Copyright © 1985 by Robert Francis and published by the University of Massachusetts Press.

"Lines Lost Among the Trees" Reprinted from *Picnic, Lightning.* Copyright © 1998 by Billy Collins and published by the University of Pittsburgh Press;

Contents

Song of the Open Road 3

Alone Looking at the Mountain 15

Eagle Plain 16

The World is too Much with Us 17

Lines Lost Among the Trees 17

Much Madness 19

I Know Not Why 19

Solitude 20

The Men That Don't Fit In 21

His Pilgrimage 22

The Summer Rain 23

The Joy of Little Things 25

On the Way 27

A Song of Winter Weather 28

The Lone Trail 30

The Pines 32

The Cremation of Sam McGee 34

The Vagabond 39

Change Should Breed Change 42

Smoke 43

Tampico 43

The Rime of the Ancient Mariner 44

A Creed 70

The Path that Leads to Nowhere 71

A Happy Life 72

Youth and Age 73

Stopping by Woods on a Snowy Evening 74

Birches 75

THE BALLAD OF THE NORTHERN LIGHTS 77
THE ROAD NOT TAKEN 89
WOODMAN, SPARE THAT TREE 90
ALONG THE ROAD 91
LYING IN A HAMMOCK AT WILLIAM DUFFY'S FARM IN PINE ISLAND, MINNESOTA 91
AFTER APPLE-PICKING 92
IF 93
THE NEGRO SPEAKS OF RIVERS 94
FAR FROM THE MADDING CROWD 95
THE CHAMBERED NAUTILUS 96
THE BIRD WITH THE COPPERY, KEEN CLAWS 97
THERE WAS A CHILD WENT FORTH 98
LEISURE 100
MY HEART LEAPS UP 101
I WANDERED LONELY AS A CLOUD 101
NO MAN IS AN ISLAND 102
THE WORLD'S ALL RIGHT 103
CUPID STUNG 106
A VAGABOND SONG 107
THE WISE OLD OWL 107
MIRACLES 108
THE COMMON ROAD 109
TO THE THAWING WIND 110
ALONE 110
MENDING WALL 111
CONSCIENCE 113
DELIGHT BECOMES PICTORIAL 114
SONG OF A MAN WHO HAS COME THROUGH 115
THE INCHCAPE ROCK 116
I THINK OVER AGAIN 118

OZYMADIAS OF EGYPT 119

FIREWARDEN ON KEARSAGE 120

THE TRAMPS 121

SONG OF MYSELF 122

I TASTE A LIQUOR NEVER BREWED 127

THE CALL OF THE WILD 128

IF A TREE COULD WANDER 130

I'M NOBODY! WHO ARE YOU? 131

NIGHT 131

ODE TO THE WEST WIND 133

STRONG BEER 136

DESIGN 137

A MILE WITH ME 138

ALTITUDE 141

Introduction

For years I have been an avid hiker and backpacker. While on backpacking trips I have always enjoyed being able to read during my down time in camp. On both short and long hiking trips the selection of suitable reading material has always been a challenge. I find that most of the good books I read tend to take me away from where I am and transport me into the story I am reading. I find being absorbed into the story of a book is highly desirable when I am reading at home; it is actually why I read. But, I find that when I am out in the wilderness, or in a new exotic location, I don't want a book to take me to "another place". I am quite happy to stay where I am. That is the purpose of the trip in the first place; it is why I came, to be where I am.

Years ago I started occasionally bringing books of poetry on my travels and I found that I enjoyed many of these poems immensely. If the poems were selected correctly, I found that this reading actually enhanced the journey instead of taking me away from it. Whether I am above tree line in the White Mountains, paddling on the Colorado River, or doing a thru hike of the Pacific Crest Trail, I want to remain where I am – having worked hard to get to some of the most beautiful spots on the planet I want to enjoy the scenery and atmosphere of where I am. I want to revel in the experience of nature and of my travels. Reading a novel, while enjoyable, always seemed to be a diversion from where I currently am. Yet reading poetry, especially poetry celebrating nature, hiking, travel, or spirituality has the opposite effect upon me. It brings me closer and more in touch with where I am at the moment.

The poems included in this book are ones selected by me primarily because I have enjoyed these poems during the course of my backpacking trips and other travels. These poems have a general theme of nature, the joys and travails of travel, and the spirit of the adventurer.

I have found that I can read and reread these poems and always gain new insights or access new feeling and thoughts depending upon my current environment. Reading a particular poem in the High Sierras of California as opposed to the deserts of Arizona can instill thoughts and experiences that are unique to each place and time.

When I first went looking for a good book of poetry geared to the backpacker or the adventure traveler I was surprised that I could not find one. Thus I decided to gather together the poems I had collected over the years and compile them into this anthology. With just a couple of exceptions the poems in this book are in the public domain. In order to keep cost to a minimum only poems where permissions to reprint the poem were freely granted were used in this collection.

Since making any money from this venture was never a goal it was decided that all proceeds from the sales of this book would be donated to the Pacific Crest Trail Association, a non-profit organization that does great work in support of a true national treasure.

I hope you enjoy the selection of poems in this anthology. It is my desire that your copy of this book becomes a little worn from the wears of travel and a little dog-eared from marking your favorites.

David (Day-Late) Thibault

Song of the Open Road

By Walt Whitman

1

Afoot and light-hearted I take to the open road,
Healthy, free, the world before me,
The long brown path before me leading wherever I choose.

Henceforth I ask not good-fortune, I myself am good-fortune,
Henceforth I whimper no more, postpone no more, need
nothing,
Done with indoor complaints, libraries, querulous criticisms,
Strong and content I travel the open road.

The earth, that is sufficient,
I do not want the constellations any nearer,
I know they are very well where they are,
I know they suffice for those who belong to them.

(Still here I carry my old delicious burdens,
I carry them, men and women, I carry them with me wherever
I go,
I swear it is impossible for me to get rid of them,
I am fill'd with them, and I will fill them in return.)

2

You road I enter upon and look around, I believe you are not
all
that is here,
I believe that much unseen is also here.

Here the profound lesson of reception, nor preference nor denial,
The black with his woolly head, the felon, the diseas'd, the illiterate person, are not denied;
The birth, the hasting after the physician, the beggar's tramp, the
drunkard's stagger, the laughing party of mechanics,
The escaped youth, the rich person's carriage, the fop, the eloping couple,
The early market-man, the hearse, the moving of furniture into the town, the return back from the town,
They pass, I also pass, any thing passes, none can be interdicted,
None but are accepted, none but shall be dear to me.

3

You air that serves me with breath to speak!
You objects that call from diffusion my meanings and give them shape!
You light that wraps me and all things in delicate equable showers!
You paths worn in the irregular hollows by the roadsides!
I believe you are latent with unseen existences, you are so dear to me.

You flagg'd walks of the cities! you strong curbs at the edges!
You ferries! you planks and posts of wharves! you timber-lined
side! you distant ships!
You rows of houses! you window-pierc'd facades! you roofs!
You porches and entrances! you copings and iron guards!
You windows whose transparent shells might expose so much!
You doors and ascending steps! you arches!
You gray stones of interminable pavements! you trodden crossings!

From all that has touch'd you I believe you have imparted to
yourselves, and now would impart the same secretly to me,
From the living and the dead you have peopled your
impassive surfaces, and the spirits thereof would be evident
and amicable with me.

4

The earth expanding right hand and left hand,
The picture alive, every part in its best light,
The music falling in where it is wanted, and stopping where it
is
not wanted,
The cheerful voice of the public road, the gay fresh sentiment
of the road.

O highway I travel, do you say to me Do not leave me?
Do you say Venture not--if you leave me you are lost?
Do you say I am already prepared, I am well-beaten and
undenied, adhere to me?

O public road, I say back I am not afraid to leave you, yet I
love you,
You express me better than I can express myself,
You shall be more to me than my poem.

I think heroic deeds were all conceiv'd in the open air, and all
free poems also,
I think I could stop here myself and do miracles,
I think whatever I shall meet on the road I shall like, and
whoever
beholds me shall like me,
I think whoever I see must be happy.

5

From this hour I ordain myself loos'd of limits and imaginary lines,
Going where I list, my own master total and absolute,
Listening to others, considering well what they say,
Pausing, searching, receiving, contemplating,
Gently, but with undeniable will, divesting myself of the holds that would hold me.

I inhale great draughts of space,
The east and the west are mine, and the north and the south are mine.

I am larger, better than I thought,
I did not know I held so much goodness.

All seems beautiful to me,
can repeat over to men and women You have done such good to me I would do the same to you,
I will recruit for myself and you as I go,
I will scatter myself among men and women as I go,
I will toss a new gladness and roughness among them,
Whoever denies me it shall not trouble me,
Whoever accepts me he or she shall be blessed and shall bless me.

6

Now if a thousand perfect men were to appear it would not amaze me,
Now if a thousand beautiful forms of women appear'd it would not astonish me.

Now I see the secret of the making of the best persons,
It is to grow in the open air and to eat and sleep with the earth.

Here a great personal deed has room,
(Such a deed seizes upon the hearts of the whole race of men,
Its effusion of strength and will overwhelms law and mocks all
authority and all argument against it.)

Here is the test of wisdom,
Wisdom is not finally tested in schools,
Wisdom cannot be pass'd from one having it to another not
having it,
Wisdom is of the soul, is not susceptible of proof, is its own
proof,
Applies to all stages and objects and qualities and is content,
Is the certainty of the reality and immortality of things, and the
excellence of things;
Something there is in the float of the sight of things that
provokes it out of the soul.

Now I re-examine philosophies and religions,
They may prove well in lecture-rooms, yet not prove at all
under the spacious clouds and along the landscape and
flowing currents.

Here is realization,
Here is a man tallied--he realizes here what he has in him,
The past, the future, majesty, love--if they are vacant of you,
you
are vacant of them.

Only the kernel of every object nourishes;
Where is he who tears off the husks for you and me?
Where is he that undoes stratagems and envelopes for you and
me?

Here is adhesiveness, it is not previously fashion'd, it is apropos;
Do you know what it is as you pass to be loved by strangers?
Do you know the talk of those turning eye-balls?

7

Here is the efflux of the soul,
The efflux of the soul comes from within through embower'd gates, ever provoking questions,
These yearnings why are they? these thoughts in the darkness why are they?
Why are there men and women that while they are nigh me the sunlight expands my blood?
Why when they leave me do my pennants of joy sink flat and lank?
Why are there trees I never walk under but large and melodious
thoughts descend upon me?
(I think they hang there winter and summer on those trees and always drop fruit as I pass;)
What is it I interchange so suddenly with strangers?
What with some driver as I ride on the seat by his side?
What with some fisherman drawing his seine by the shore as I walk by and pause?
What gives me to be free to a woman's and man's good-will? what gives them to be free to mine?

8

The efflux of the soul is happiness, here is happiness,
I think it pervades the open air, waiting at all times,
Now it flows unto us, we are rightly charged.

Here rises the fluid and attaching character,

The fluid and attaching character is the freshness and
sweetness of man and woman,
(The herbs of the morning sprout no fresher and sweeter every
day out of the roots of themselves, than it sprouts fresh and
sweet continually out of itself.)

Toward the fluid and attaching character exudes the sweat of
the
love of young and old,
From it falls distill'd the charm that mocks beauty and
attainments,
Toward it heaves the shuddering longing ache of contact.

9

Allons! whoever you are come travel with me!
Traveling with me you find what never tires.

The earth never tires,
The earth is rude, silent, incomprehensible at first, Nature is
rude and incomprehensible at first,
Be not discouraged, keep on, there are divine things well
envelop'd,
I swear to you there are divine things more beautiful than
words can tell.

Allons! we must not stop here,
However sweet these laid-up stores, however convenient this
dwelling we cannot remain here,
However shelter'd this port and however calm these waters
we must not anchor here,
However welcome the hospitality that surrounds us we are
permitted to receive it but a little while.

10

Allons! the inducements shall be greater,
We will sail pathless and wild seas,
We will go where winds blow, waves dash, and the Yankee clipper speeds by under full sail.

Allons! with power, liberty, the earth, the elements,
Health, defiance, gayety, self-esteem, curiosity;
Allons! from all formules!
From your formules, O bat-eyed and materialistic priests.

The stale cadaver blocks up the passage--the burial waits no longer.

Allons! yet take warning!
He traveling with me needs the best blood, thews, endurance,
None may come to the trial till he or she bring courage and health,
Come not here if you have already spent the best of yourself,
Only those may come who come in sweet and determin'd bodies,
No diseas'd person, no rum-drinker or venereal taint is permitted here.

(I and mine do not convince by arguments, similes, rhymes,
We convince by our presence.)

11

Listen! I will be honest with you,
I do not offer the old smooth prizes, but offer rough new prizes,
These are the days that must happen to you:
You shall not heap up what is call'd riches,
You shall scatter with lavish hand all that you earn or achieve,
You but arrive at the city to which you were destin'd, you hardly

settle yourself to satisfaction before you are call'd by an
irresistible call to depart,
You shall be treated to the ironical smiles and mockings of
those
who remain behind you,
What beckonings of love you receive you shall only answer
with
passionate kisses of parting,
You shall not allow the hold of those who spread their reach'd
hands toward you.

12

Allons! after the great Companions, and to belong to them!
They too are on the road--they are the swift and majestic men--
they are the greatest women,
Enjoyers of calms of seas and storms of seas,
Sailors of many a ship, walkers of many a mile of land,
Habitues of many distant countries, habitues of far-distant
dwellings,
Trusters of men and women, observers of cities, solitary
toilers,
Pausers and contemplators of tufts, blossoms, shells of the
shore,
Dancers at wedding-dances, kissers of brides, tender helpers
of
children, bearers of children,
Soldiers of revolts, standers by gaping graves, lowerers-down
of coffins,
Journeyers over consecutive seasons, over the years, the
curious
years each emerging from that which preceded it,
Journeyers as with companions, namely their own diverse
phases,
Forth-steppers from the latent unrealized baby-days,
Journeyers gayly with their own youth, journeyers with their

bearded and well-grain'd manhood,
Journeyers with their womanhood, ample, unsurpass'd, content,
Journeyers with their own sublime old age of manhood or womanhood,
Old age, calm, expanded, broad with the haughty breadth of the universe,
Old age, flowing free with the delicious near-by freedom of death.

13

Allons! to that which is endless as it was beginningless,
To undergo much, tramps of days, rests of nights,
To merge all in the travel they tend to, and the days and nights they tend to,
Again to merge them in the start of superior journeys,
To see nothing anywhere but what you may reach it and pass it,
To conceive no time, however distant, but what you may reach it and pass it,
To look up or down no road but it stretches and waits for you, however long but it stretches and waits for you,
To see no being, not God's or any, but you also go thither,
To see no possession but you may possess it, enjoying all without labor or purchase, abstracting the feast yet not abstracting one particle of it,
To take the best of the farmer's farm and the rich man's elegant villa, and the chaste blessings of the well-married couple, and the fruits of orchards and flowers of gardens,
To take to your use out of the compact cities as you pass through,
To carry buildings and streets with you afterward wherever you go,
To gather the minds of men out of their brains as you encounter

them, to gather the love out of their hearts,
To take your lovers on the road with you, for all that you leave them behind you,
To know the universe itself as a road, as many roads, as roads for traveling souls.

All parts away for the progress of souls,
All religion, all solid things, arts, governments--all that was or is apparent upon this globe or any globe, falls into niches and corners before the procession of souls along the grand roads of the universe.

Of the progress of the souls of men and women along the grand roads of the universe, all other progress is the needed emblem and sustenance.

Forever alive, forever forward,
Stately, solemn, sad, withdrawn, baffled, mad, turbulent, feeble, dissatisfied,
Desperate, proud, fond, sick, accepted by men, rejected by men,
They go! they go! I know that they go, but I know not where they go,
But I know that they go toward the best--toward something great.

Whoever you are, come forth! or man or woman come forth!
You must not stay sleeping and dallying there in the house, though you built it, or though it has been built for you.

Out of the dark confinement! out from behind the screen!
It is useless to protest, I know all and expose it.

Behold through you as bad as the rest,
Through the laughter, dancing, dining, supping, of people,
Inside of dresses and ornaments, inside of those wash'd and trimm'd faces,
Behold a secret silent loathing and despair.

No husband, no wife, no friend, trusted to hear the confession,
Another self, a duplicate of every one, skulking and hiding it goes,
Formless and wordless through the streets of the cities, polite and bland in the parlors,
In the cars of railroads, in steamboats, in the public assembly,
Home to the houses of men and women, at the table, in the bedroom, everywhere,
Smartly attired, countenance smiling, form upright, death under the breast-bones, hell under the skull-bones,
Under the broadcloth and gloves, under the ribbons and artificial flowers,
Keeping fair with the customs, speaking not a syllable of itself,
Speaking of any thing else but never of itself.

14

Allons! through struggles and wars!
The goal that was named cannot be countermanded.

Have the past struggles succeeded?
What has succeeded? yourself? your nation? Nature?
Now understand me well--it is provided in the essence of things that from any fruition of success, no matter what, shall come forth something to make a greater struggle necessary.

My call is the call of battle, I nourish active rebellion,

He going with me must go well arm'd,
He going with me goes often with spare diet, poverty, angry enemies, desertions.

15

Allons! the road is before us!
It is safe--I have tried it--my own feet have tried it well--be not detain'd!
Let the paper remain on the desk unwritten, and the book on the shelf unopen'd!
Let the tools remain in the workshop! let the money remain unearn'd!
Let the school stand! mind not the cry of the teacher!
Let the preacher preach in his pulpit! let the lawyer plead in the court, and the judge expound the law.

Camerado, I give you my hand!
I give you my love more precious than money,
I give you myself before preaching or law;
Will you give me yourself? will you come travel with me?
Shall we stick by each other as long as we live?

Alone Looking at the Mountain

By Li Po

All the birds have flown up and gone;
A lonely cloud floats leisurely by.
We never tire of looking at each other -
Only the mountain and I.

Eagle Plain

By Robert Francis

The American eagle is not aware he is
the American eagle. He is never tempted
to look modest.

When orators advertise the American eagle's
virtues, the American eagle is not listening.
This is his virtue.

He is somewhere else, he is mountains away
but even if he were near he would never
make an audience.

The American eagle never says he will serve
if drafted, will dutifully serve etc. He is
not at our service.

If we have honored him we have honored one
who unequivocally honors himself by
overlooking us.

He does not know the meaning of magnificent.
Perhaps we do not altogether either
who cannot touch him.

The World is too Much with Us

By William Wordsworth

The world is too much with us; late and soon,
  Getting and spending, we lay waste our powers;
  Little we see in Nature that is ours.
We have given our hearts away, a sordid boon!
This sea, that bares her bosom to the moon,
  The winds that will be howling at all hours,
  And are up-gathered now like sleeping flowers--
For this, for everything, we are out of tune;
It moves us not. Great God! I'd rather be
  A pagan, suckled in a creed outworn,
So might I, standing on this pleasant lea,
  Have glimpses that would make me less forlorn;
Have sight of Proteus, rising from the sea,
  Or hear old Triton blow his wreathed horn.

Lines Lost Among the Trees

By Billy Collins

These are not the lines that came to me
while walking in the woods
with no pen
and nothing to write on anyway.

They are gone forever,
a handful of coins
dropped through the grate of memory,
along with the ingenious mnemonic

I devised to hold them in place-
all gone and forgotten
before I had returned to the clearing of lawn
in back of our quiet house

with its jars jammed with pens,
its notebooks and reams of blank paper,
its desk and soft lamp,
its table and the light from its windows.

So this is my elegy for them,
those six or eight exhalations,
the braided rope of the syntax,
the jazz of the timing,

and the little insight at the end
wagging like the short tail
of a perfectly obedient spaniel
sitting by the door.

This is my envoy to nothing
where I say Go, little poem-
not out into the world of strangers' eyes,
but off to some airy limbo,

home to lost epics,
unremembered names,
and fugitive dreams
such as the one I had last night,

which, like a fantastic city in pencil,
erased itself
in the bright morning air
just as I was waking up.

Much Madness

By Emily Dickinson

Much madness is divinest sense
To a discerning eye;
Much sense the starkest madness.
'T is the majority
In this, as all, prevails.
Assent, and you are sane;
Demur,—you 're straightway dangerous,
And handled with a chain.

I Know Not Why

By Morris Rosenfeld

I lift mine eyes against the sky,
The clouds are weeping, so am I;
I lift mine eyes again on high,
The sun is smiling, so am I.
Why do I smile? Why do I weep?
I do not know; it lies too deep.

I hear the winds of autumn sigh,
They break my heart, they make me cry;
I hear the birds of lovely spring,
My hopes revive, I help them sing.
Why do I sing? Why do I cry?
It lies so deep, I know not why.

Solitude

By Alexander Pope

Happy the man, whose wish and care
A few paternal acres bound,
Content to breathe his native air
        In his own ground.

Whose herds with milk, whose fields with bread,
Whose flocks supply him with attire;
Whose trees in summer yield him shade,
        In winter fire.

Blest, who can unconcern'dly find
Hours, days, and years slide soft away
In health of body, peace of mind,
        Quiet by day,

Sound sleep by night; study and ease
Together mixt, sweet recreation,
And innocence, which most does please
        With meditation.

Thus let me live, unseen, unknown;
Thus unlamented let me die;
Steal from the world, and not a stone
        Tell where I lie.

The Men That Don't Fit In

By Robert William Service

There's a race of men that don't fit in,
  A race that can't stay still;
So they break the hearts of kith and kin,
  And they roam the world at will.
They range the field and they rove the flood,
  And they climb the mountain's crest;
Theirs is the curse of the gypsy blood,
  And they don't know how to rest.

If they just went straight they might go far;

  They are strong and brave and true;
But they're always tired of the things that are,
  And they want the strange and new.
They say: "Could I find my proper groove,
  What a deep mark I would make!"
So they chop and change, and each fresh move
  Is only a fresh mistake.

And each forgets, as he strips and runs
  With a brilliant, fitful pace,
It's the steady, quiet, plodding ones
  Who win in the lifelong race.
And each forgets that his youth has fled,
  Forgets that his prime is past,
Till he stands one day, with a hope that's dead,
  In the glare of the truth at last.

He has failed, he has failed; he has missed his chance;

He has just done things by half.
Life's been a jolly good joke on him,
And now is the time to laugh.
Ha, ha! He is one of the Legion Lost;
He was never meant to win;
He's a rolling stone, and it's bred in the bone;
He's a man who won't fit in.

His Pilgrimage

By Sir Walter Raleigh

Give me my scallop-shell of quiet,
My staff of faith to walk upon,
My scrip of joy, immortal diet,
My bottle of salvation,
My gown of glory, hope's true gage;
And thus I'll take my pilgrimage.

Blood must be my body's balmer;
No other balm will there be given:
Whilst my soul, like quiet palmer,
Travelleth towards the land of heaven;
Over the silver mountains,
Where spring the nectar fountains;
There will I kiss
The bowl of bliss;
And drink mine everlasting fill
Upon every milken hill.
My soul will be a-dry before;
But, after, it will thirst no more.

The Summer Rain

By Henry David Thoreau

My books I'd fain cast off, I cannot read,
'Twixt every page my thoughts go stray at large
Down in the meadow, where is richer feed,
And will not mind to hit their proper targe.
Plutarch was good, and so was Homer too,
Our Shakespeare's life were rich to live again,
What Plutarch read, that was not good nor true,
Nor Shakespeare's books, unless his books were men.

Here while I lie beneath this walnut bough,
What care I for the Greeks or for Troy town,
If juster battles are enacted now
Between the ants upon this hummock's crown?

Bid Homer wait till I the issue learn,
If red or black the gods will favor most,
Or yonder Ajax will the phalanx turn,
Struggling to heave some rock against the host.

Tell Shakespeare to attend some leisure hour,
For now I've business with this drop of dew,
And see you not, the clouds prepare a shower--
I'll meet him shortly when the sky is blue.

This bed of herd's grass and wild oats was spread
Last year with nicer skill than monarchs use.
A clover tuft is pillow for my head,
And violets quite overtop my shoes.

And now the cordial clouds have shut all in,
And gently swells the wind to say all's well;
The scattered drops are falling fast and thin,
Some in the pool, some in the flower-bell.

I am well drenched upon my bed of oats;
But see that globe come rolling down its stem,
Now like a lonely planet there it floats,
And now it sinks into my garment's hem.

Drip drip the trees for all the country round,
And richness rare distills from every bough;
The wind alone it is makes every sound,
Shaking down crystals on the leaves below.

For shame the sun will never show himself,
Who could not with his beams e'er melt me so;
My dripping locks--they would become an elf,
Who in a beaded coat does gayly go.

The Joy of Little Things

By Robert William Service

It's good the great green earth to roam,
Where sights of awe the soul inspire;
But oh, it's best, the coming home,
The crackle of one's own hearth-fire!
You've hob-nobbed with the solemn Past;
You've seen the pageantry of kings;
Yet oh, how sweet to gain at last
The peace and rest of Little Things!

Perhaps you're counted with the Great;
You strain and strive with mighty men;
Your hand is on the helm of State;
Colossus-like you stride . . . and then
There comes a pause, a shining hour,
A dog that leaps, a hand that clings:
O Titan, turn from pomp and power;
Give all your heart to Little Things.

Go couch you childwise in the grass,
Believing it's some jungle strange,
Where mighty monsters peer and pass,
Where beetles roam and spiders range.
'Mid gloom and gleam of leaf and blade,
What dragons rasp their painted wings!

O magic world of shine and shade!
O beauty land of Little Things!

I sometimes wonder, after all,
Amid this tangled web of fate,
If what is great may not be small,
And what is small may not be great.
So wondering I go my way,
Yet in my heart contentment sings . . .
O may I ever see, I pray,
God's grace and love in Little Things.

So give to me, I only beg,
A little roof to call my own,
A little cider in the keg,
A little meat upon the bone;
A little garden by the sea,
A little boat that dips and swings . . .
Take wealth, take fame, but leave to me,
O Lord of Life, just Little Things.

On the Way

By Carl Sandburg

Little one, you have been buzzing in the books,
Flittering in the newspapers and drinking beer with lawyers
And amid the educated men of the clubs you have been getting an earful of speech from trained tongues.
Take an earful from me once, go with me on a hike
Along sand stretches on the great inland sea here
And while the eastern breeze blows on us and the restless surge
Of the lake waves on the breakwater breaks with an ever fresh monotone,
Let us ask ourselves: What is truth? what do you or I know?
How much do the wisest of the world's men know about where the massed human procession is going?

You have heard the mob laughed at?
I ask you: Is not the mob rough as the mountains are rough?
And all things human rise from the mob and relapse and rise again as rain to the sea.

A Song of Winter Weather

By Robert William Service

It isn't the foe that we fear;
  It isn't the bullets that whine;
It isn't the business career
  Of a shell, or the bust of a mine;
It isn't the snipers who seek
  To nip our young hopes in the bud:
No, it isn't the guns,
And it isn't the Huns --
  It's the MUD,
          MUD,
               MUD.

It isn't the melee we mind.
That often is rather good fun.
  It isn't the shrapnel we find
Obtrusive when rained by the ton;
  It isn't the bounce of the bombs
That gives us a positive pain:
  It's the strafing we get
When the weather is wet --
  It's the RAIN,
          RAIN,
               RAIN.

It isn't because we lack grit
   We shrink from the horrors of war.
We don't mind the battle a bit;
   In fact that is what we are for;
It isn't the rum-jars and things
   Make us wish we were back in the fold:
It's the fingers that freeze
In the boreal breeze --
   It's the COLD,
            COLD,
               COLD.

Oh, the rain, the mud, and the cold,
   The cold, the mud, and the rain;
With weather at zero it's hard for a hero
   From language that's rude to refrain.
With porridgy muck to the knees,
   With sky that's a-pouring a flood,
Sure the worst of our foes
Are the pains and the woes
   Of the RAIN,
         THE COLD,
            AND THE MUD.

The Lone Trail

By Robert William Service

Ye who know the Lone Trail fain would follow it,
Though it lead to glory or the darkness of the pit.
Ye who take the Lone Trail, bid your love good-by;
The Lone Trail, the Lone Trail follow till you die.

The trails of the world be countless, and most of the trails be tried;
You tread on the heels of the many, till you come where the ways divide;
And one lies safe in the sunlight, and the other is dreary and wan,
Yet you look aslant at the Lone Trail, and the Lone Trail lures you on.
And somehow you're sick of the highway, with its noise and its easy needs,
And you seek the risk of the by-way, and you reck not where it leads.
And sometimes it leads to the desert, and the togue swells out of the mouth,
And you stagger blind to the mirage, to die in the mocking drouth.
And sometimes it leads to the mountain, to the light of the lone camp-fire,
And you gnaw your belt in the anguish of hunger-goded desire.

And sometimes it leads to the Southland, to the swamp where the orchid glows,

And you rave to your grave with the fever, and they rob the corpse for its clothes.

And sometimes it leads to the Northland, and the scurvy softens your bones,

And your flesh dints in like putty, and you spit out your teeth like stones.

And sometimes it leads to a coral reef in the wash of a weedy sea,

And you sit and stare at the empty glare where the gulls wait greedily.

And sometimes it leads to an Arctic trail, and the snows where your torn feet freeze,

And you whittle away the useless clay, and crawl on your hands and knees.

Often it leads to the dead-pit; always it leads to pain;

By the bones of your brothers ye know it, but oh, to follow you're fain.

By your bones they will follow behind you, till the ways of the world are made plain.

Bid good-by to sweetheart, bid good-by to friend;

The Lone Trail, the Lone Trail follow to the end.

Tarry not, and fear not, chosen of the true;

Lover of the Lone Trail, the Lone Trail waits for you.

The Pines

By Robert William Service

We sleep in the sleep of ages, the bleak, barbarian pines;
The gray moss drapes us like sages, and closer we lock our lines,
And deeper we clutch through the gelid gloom where never a sunbeam shines.

On the flanks of the storm-gored ridges are our black battalions massed;
We surge in a host to the sullen coast, and we sing in the ocean blast;
From empire of sea to empire of snow we grip our empire fast.

To the niggard lands were we driven, 'twixt desert and floes are we penned;
To us was the Northland given, ours to stronghold and defend;

Ours till the world be riven in the crash of the utter end;

Ours from the bleak beginning, through the aeons of death-like sleep;
Ours from the shock when the naked rock was hurled from the hissing deep;
Ours through the twilight ages of weary glacier creep.

Wind of the East, Wind of the West, wandering to and fro,
Chant your songs in our topmost boughs, that the sons of men may know
The peerless pine was the first to come, and the pine will be last to go!

We pillar the halls of perfumed gloom; we plume where the eagles soar;
The North-wind swoops from the brooding Pole, and our ancients crash and roar;
But where one falls from the crumbling walls shoots up a hardy score.

We spring from the gloom of the canyon's womb; in the valley's lap we lie;
From the white foam-fringe, where the breakers cringe to the peaks that tusk the sky,
We climb, and we peer in the crag-locked mere that gleams like a golden eye.

Gain to the verge of the hog-back ridge where the vision ranges free:
Pines and pines and the shadow of pines as far as the eye can see;
A steadfast legion of stalwart knights in dominant empery.

Sun, moon and stars give answer; shall we not staunchly stand,
Even as now, forever, wards of the wilder strand,
Sentinels of the stillness, lords of the last, lone land?

The Cremation of Sam McGee

By Robert William Service

There are strange things done in the midnight sun
  By the men who moil for gold;
The Arctic trails have their secret tales
  That would make your blood run cold;
The Northern Lights have seen queer sights,
  But the queerest they ever did see
Was that night on the marge of Lake Lebarge
  I cremated Sam McGee.

Now Sam McGee was from Tennessee, where the cotton blooms and blows.
Why he left his home in the South to roam 'round the Pole, God only knows.
He was always cold, but the land of gold seemed to hold him like a spell;
Though he'd often say in his homely way that he'd "sooner live in hell".

On a Christmas Day we were mushing our way over the Dawson trail.
Talk of your cold! through the parka's fold it stabbed like a driven nail.
If our eyes we'd close, then the lashes froze till sometimes we couldn't see;

It wasn't much fun, but the only one to whimper was Sam McGee.

And that very night, as we lay packed tight in our robes beneath the snow,

And the dogs were fed, and the stars o'erhead were dancing heel and toe,

He turned to me, and "Cap," says he, "I'll cash in this trip, I guess;

And if I do, I'm asking that you won't refuse my last request."

Well, he seemed so low that I couldn't say no; then he says with a sort of moan:

"It's the cursed cold, and it's got right hold till I'm chilled clean through to the bone.

Yet 'tain't being dead -- it's my awful dread of the icy grave that pains;

So I want you to swear that, foul or fair, you'll cremate my last remains."

A pal's last need is a thing to heed, so I swore I would not fail;

And we started on at the streak of dawn; but God! he looked ghastly pale.

He crouched on the sleigh, and he raved all day of his home in Tennessee;

And before nightfall a corpse was all that was left of Sam McGee.

There wasn't a breath in that land of death, and I hurried, horror-driven,

With a corpse half hid that I couldn't get rid, because of a promise given;

It was lashed to the sleigh, and it seemed to say:

"You may tax your brawn and brains,

But you promised true, and it's up to you to cremate those last remains."

Now a promise made is a debt unpaid, and the trail has its own stern code.

In the days to come, though my lips were dumb, in my heart how I cursed that load.

In the long, long night, by the lone firelight, while the huskies, round in a ring,

Howled out their woes to the homeless snows -- O God! how I loathed the thing.

And every day that quiet clay seemed to heavy and heavier grow;

And on I went, though the dogs were spent and the grub was getting low;

The trail was bad, and I felt half mad, but I swore I would not give in;

And I'd often sing to the hateful thing, and it hearkened with a grin.

Till I came to the marge of Lake Lebarge, and a derelict there lay;

It was jammed in the ice, but I saw in a trice it was called the "Alice May".

And I looked at it, and I thought a bit, and I looked at my frozen chum;

Then "Here," said I, with a sudden cry, "is my cre-ma-tor-eum."

Some planks I tore from the cabin floor, and I lit the boiler fire;
Some coal I found that was lying around, and I heaped the fuel higher;
The flames just soared, and the furnace roared -- such a blaze you seldom see;
And I burrowed a hole in the glowing coal, and I stuffed in Sam McGee.

Then I made a hike, for I didn't like to hear him sizzle so;
And the heavens scowled, and the huskies howled, and the wind began to blow.
It was icy cold, but the hot sweat rolled down my cheeks, and I don't know why;
And the greasy smoke in an inky cloak went streaking down the sky.

I do not know how long in the snow I wrestled with grisly fear;
But the stars came out and they danced about ere again I ventured near;
I was sick with dread, but I bravely said: "I'll just take a peep inside.
I guess he's cooked, and it's time I looked"; . . . then the door I opened wide.

And there sat Sam, looking cool and calm, in the heart of the furnace roar;

And he wore a smile you could see a mile, and he said: "Please close that door.

It's fine in here, but I greatly fear you'll let in the cold and storm --

Since I left Plumtree, down in Tennessee, it's the first time I've been warm."

There are strange things done in the midnight sun
   By the men who moil for gold;
The Arctic trails have their secret tales
   That would make your blood run cold;
The Northern Lights have seen queer sights,
   But the queerest they ever did see
Was that night on the marge of Lake Lebarge
   I cremated Sam McGee.

The Vagabond

By Henry Lawson

White handkerchiefs wave from the short black pier
    As we glide to the grand old sea --
But the song of my heart is for none to hear
    If one of them waves for me.
A roving, roaming life is mine,
    Ever by field or flood --
For not far back in my father's line
    Was a dash of the Gipsy blood.

Flax and tussock and fern,
    Gum and mulga and sand,
Reef and palm -- but my fancies turn
    Ever away from land;
Strange wild cities in ancient state,
    Range and river and tree,
Snow and ice. But my star of fate
    Is ever across the sea.

A god-like ride on a thundering sea,
    When all but the stars are blind --
A desperate race from Eternity
    With a gale-and-a-half behind.
A jovial spree in the cabin at night,
    A song on the rolling deck,
A lark ashore with the ships in sight,
    Till -- a wreck goes down with a wreck.

A smoke and a yarn on the deck by day,
    When life is a waking dream,
And care and trouble so far away

That out of your life they seem.
A roving spirit in sympathy,
Who has travelled the whole world o'er --
My heart forgets, in a week at sea,
The trouble of years on shore.

A rolling stone! -- 'tis a saw for slaves --
Philosophy false as old --
Wear out or break 'neath the feet of knaves,
Or rot in your bed of mould!
But I'D rather trust to the darkest skies
And the wildest seas that roar,
Or die, where the stars of Nations rise,
In the stormy clouds of war.

Cleave to your country, home, and friends,
Die in a sordid strife --
You can count your friends on your finger ends
In the critical hours of life.
Sacrifice all for the family's sake,
Bow to their selfish rule!
Slave till your big soft heart they break --
The heart of the family fool.

Domestic quarrels, and family spite,
And your Native Land may be
Controlled by custom, but, come what might,
The rest of the world for me.
I'd sail with money, or sail without! --
If your love be forced from home,
And you dare enough, and your heart be stout,
The world is your own to roam.

I've never a love that can sting my pride,
Nor a friend to prove untrue;
For I leave my love ere the turning tide,

And my friends are all too new.
The curse of the Powers on a peace like ours,
With its greed and its treachery --
A stranger's hand, and a stranger land,
And the rest of the world for me!

But why be bitter? The world is cold
To one with a frozen heart;
New friends are often so like the old,
They seem of the past a part --
As a better part of the past appears,
When enemies, parted long,
Are come together in kinder years,
With their better nature strong.

I had a friend, ere my first ship sailed,
A friend that I never deserved --
For the selfish strain in my blood prevailed
As soon as my turn was served.
And the memory haunts my heart with shame --
Or, rather, the pride that's there;
In different guises, but soul the same,
I meet him everywhere.

I had a chum. When the times were tight
We starved in Australian scrubs;
We froze together in parks at night,
And laughed together in pubs.
And I often hear a laugh like his
From a sense of humour keen,
And catch a glimpse in a passing phiz
Of his broad, good-humoured grin.

And I had a love -- 'twas a love to prize --
But I never went back again . . .
I have seen the light of her kind brown eyes

In many a face since then.
The sailors say 'twill be rough to-night,
As they fasten the hatches down,
The south is black, and the bar is white,
And the drifting smoke is brown.
The gold has gone from the western haze,
The sea-birds circle and swarm --
But we shall have plenty of sunny days,
And little enough of storm.

The hill is hiding the short black pier,
As the last white signal's seen;
The points run in, and the houses veer,
And the great bluff stands between.
So darkness swallows each far white speck
On many a wharf and quay.
The night comes down on a restless deck, --
Grim cliffs -- and -- The Open Sea!

Change Should Breed Change

By William Drummond

New doth the sun appear,
The mountains' snows decay,
Crown'd with frail flowers forth comes the baby year.
My soul, time posts away;
And thou yet in that frost
Which flower and fruit hath lost,
As if all here immortal were, dost stay.
For shame! thy powers awake,
Look to that Heaven which never night makes black,
And there at that immortal sun's bright rays,
Deck thee with flowers which fear not rage of days!

Smoke

By Henry David Thoreau

Light-wingèd Smoke, Icarian bird,
Melting thy pinions in thy upward flight,
Lark without song, and messenger of dawn,
Circling above the hamlets as thy nest;
Or else, departing dream, and shadowy form
Of midnight vision, gathering up thy skirts;
By night star-veiling, and by day
Darkening the light and blotting out the sun;
Go thou my incense upward from this hearth,
And ask the gods to pardon this clear flame.

Tampico

By Grace Hazard Conkling

Oh, cut me reeds to blow upon,
Or gather me a star,
But leave the sultry passion-flowers
Growing where they are.

I fear their sombre yellow deeps,
Their whirling fringe of black,
And he who gives a passion-flower
Always asks it back.

The Rime of the Ancient Mariner

By Samuel Taylor Coleridge

PART I

An ancient Mariner meeteth three gallants bidden to a wedding feast, and detaineth one.

It is an ancient Mariner,
And he stoppeth one of three.
'By thy long beard and glittering eye,
Now wherefore stopp'st thou me?

The Bridegroom's doors are opened wide,
And I am next of kin;
The guests are met, the feast is set:
May'st hear the merry din.'

He holds him with his skinny hand,
'There was a ship,' quoth he.
'Hold off! unhand me, grey-beard loon!'
Eftsoons his hand dropt he.

The Wedding-Guest is spell-bound by the eye of the old seafaring man, and constrained to hear his tale.

He holds him with his glittering eye--
The Wedding-Guest stood still,
And listens like a three years' child:
The Mariner hath his will.

The Wedding-Guest sat on a stone:
He cannot choose but hear;

And thus spake on that ancient man,
The bright-eyed Mariner.

'The ship was cheer'd, the harbour clear'd,
Merrily did we drop
Below the kirk, below the hill,
Below the lighthouse top.

The Mariner tells how the ship sailed southward with a good wind and fair weather, till it reached the Line.

The Sun came up upon the left,
Out of the sea came he!
And he shone bright, and on the right
Went down into the sea.

Higher and higher every day,
Till over the mast at noon----'
The Wedding-Guest here beat his breast,
For he heard the loud bassoon.

The Wedding-Guest heareth the bridal music; but the Mariner continueth his tale.

The bride hath paced into the hall,
Red as a rose is she;
Nodding their heads before her goes
The merry minstrelsy.

The Wedding-Guest he beat his breast,
Yet he cannot choose but hear;
And thus spake on that ancient man,
The bright-eyed Mariner.

The ship drawn by a storm toward the South Pole.

'And now the Storm-blast came, and he
Was tyrannous and strong:
He struck with his o'ertaking wings,
And chased us south along.

With sloping masts and dipping prow,
As who pursued with yell and blow
Still treads the shadow of his foe,
And forward bends his head,
The ship drove fast, loud roar'd the blast,
The southward aye we fled.

And now there came both mist and snow,
And it grew wondrous cold:
And ice, mast-high, came floating by,
As green as emerald.

The land of ice, and of fearful sounds, where no living thing was to be seen.

And through the drifts the snowy clifts
Did send a dismal sheen:
Nor shapes of men nor beasts we ken--
The ice was all between.

The ice was here, the ice was there,
The ice was all around:
It crack'd and growl'd, and roar'd and howl'd,
Like noises in a swound!

Till a great sea-bird, called the Albatross, came through the snow-fog, and was received with great joy and hospitality.

At length did cross an Albatross,
Thorough the fog it came;
As if it had been a Christian soul,

We hail'd it in God's name.

It ate the food it ne'er had eat,
And round and round it flew.
The ice did split with a thunder-fit;
The helmsman steer'd us through!

And lo! the Albatross proveth a bird of good omen, and followeth the ship as it returned northward through fog and floating ice.

And a good south wind sprung up behind;
The Albatross did follow,
And every day, for food or play,
Came to the mariners' hollo!

In mist or cloud, on mast or shroud,
It perch'd for vespers nine;
Whiles all the night, through fog-smoke white,
Glimmer'd the white moonshine.'

The ancient Mariner inhospitably killeth the pious bird of good omen.

'God save thee, ancient Mariner!
From the fiends, that plague thee thus!--
Why look'st thou so?'--'With my crossbow
I shot the Albatross.

PART II

'The Sun now rose upon the right:
Out of the sea came he,
Still hid in mist, and on the left
Went down into the sea.

And the good south wind still blew behind,

But no sweet bird did follow,
Nor any day for food or play
Came to the mariners' hollo!

His shipmates cry out against the ancient Mariner for killing the bird of good luck.

And I had done an hellish thing,
And it would work 'em woe:
For all averr'd, I had kill'd the bird
That made the breeze to blow.
Ah wretch! said they, the bird to slay,
That made the breeze to blow!

But when the fog cleared off, they justify the same, and thus make themselves accomplices in the crime.

Nor dim nor red, like God's own head,
The glorious Sun uprist:
Then all averr'd, I had kill'd the bird
That brought the fog and mist.
'Twas right, said they, such birds to slay,
That bring the fog and mist.

The fair breeze continues; the ship enters the Pacific Ocean, and sails northward, even till it reaches the Line.

The fair breeze blew, the white foam flew,
The furrow follow'd free;
We were the first that ever burst
Into that silent sea.

The ship hath been suddenly becalmed.

Down dropt the breeze, the sails dropt down,
'Twas sad as sad could be;

And we did speak only to break
The silence of the sea!

All in a hot and copper sky,
The bloody Sun, at noon,
Right up above the mast did stand,
No bigger than the Moon.

Day after day, day after day,
We stuck, nor breath nor motion;
As idle as a painted ship
Upon a painted ocean.

And the Albatross begins to be avenged.

Water, water, everywhere,
And all the boards did shrink;
Water, water, everywhere,
Nor any drop to drink.

The very deep did rot: O Christ!
That ever this should be!
Yea, slimy things did crawl with legs
Upon the slimy sea.

About, about, in reel and rout
The death-fires danced at night;
The water, like a witch's oils,
Burnt green, and blue, and white.

A Spirit had followed them; one of the invisible inhabitants of this planet, neither departed souls nor angels; concerning whom the learned Jew, Josephus, and the Platonic Constantinopolitan, Michael Psellus,
may be consulted. They are very numerous, and there is no climate or element without one or more.

And some in dreams assured were
Of the Spirit that plagued us so;
Nine fathom deep he had followed us
From the land of mist and snow.

And every tongue, through utter drought,
Was wither'd at the root;
We could not speak, no more than if
We had been choked with soot.

The shipmates in their sore distress, would fain throw the whole guilt on the ancient Mariner: in sign whereof they hang the dead sea-bird round his neck.

Ah! well a-day! what evil looks
Had I from old and young!
Instead of the cross, the Albatross
About my neck was hung.

PART III

'There passed a weary time. Each throat
Was parch'd, and glazed each eye.
A weary time! a weary time!
How glazed each weary eye!
When looking westward, I beheld
A something in the sky.

The ancient Mariner beholdeth a sign in the element afar off.

At first it seem'd a little speck,
And then it seem'd a mist;
It moved and moved, and took at last
A certain shape, I wist.

A speck, a mist, a shape, I wist!
And still it near'd and near'd:
As if it dodged a water-sprite,
It plunged, and tack'd, and veer'd.

At its nearer approach, it seemeth him to be a ship; and at a dear ransom he freeth his speech from the bonds of thirst.

With throats unslaked, with black lips baked,
We could nor laugh nor wail;
Through utter drought all dumb we stood!
I bit my arm, I suck'd the blood,
And cried, A sail! a sail!

A flash of joy;

With throats unslaked, with black lips baked,
Agape they heard me call:
Gramercy! they for joy did grin,
And all at once their breath drew in,
As they were drinking all.

And horror follows. For can it be a ship that comes onward without wind or tide?

See! see! (I cried) she tacks no more!
Hither to work us weal--
Without a breeze, without a tide,
She steadies with upright keel!

The western wave was all aflame,
The day was wellnigh done!
Almost upon the western wave
Rested the broad, bright Sun;
When that strange shape drove suddenly
Betwixt us and the Sun.

It seemeth him but the skeleton of a ship.

And straight the Sun was fleck'd with bars
(Heaven's Mother send us grace!),
As if through a dungeon-grate he peer'd
With broad and burning face.

Alas! (thought I, and my heart beat loud)
How fast she nears and nears!
Are those her sails that glance in the Sun,
Like restless gossameres?

And its ribs are seen as bars on the face of the setting Sun. The Spectre-Woman and her Death-mate, and no other on board the skeleton ship. Like vessel, like crew!

Are those her ribs through which the Sun
Did peer, as through a grate?
And is that Woman all her crew?
Is that a Death? and are there two?
Is Death that Woman's mate?

Her lips were red, her looks were free,
Her locks were yellow as gold:
Her skin was as white as leprosy,
The Nightmare Life-in-Death was she,
Who thicks man's blood with cold.

Death and Life-in-Death have diced for the ship's crew, and she (the latter) winneth the ancient Mariner.

The naked hulk alongside came,
And the twain were casting dice;
"The game is done! I've won! I've won!"
Quoth she, and whistles thrice.

No twilight within the courts of the Sun.

The Sun's rim dips; the stars rush out:
At one stride comes the dark;
With far-heard whisper, o'er the sea,
Off shot the spectre-bark.

We listen'd and look'd sideways up!
Fear at my heart, as at a cup,
My life-blood seem'd to sip!
The stars were dim, and thick the night,
The steersman's face by his lamp gleam'd white;
From the sails the dew did drip--
Till clomb above the eastern bar
The horned Moon, with one bright star
Within the nether tip.

At the rising of the Moon,
One after another,

One after one, by the star-dogg'd Moon,
Too quick for groan or sigh,
Each turn'd his face with a ghastly pang,
And cursed me with his eye.

His shipmates drop down dead.

Four times fifty living men
(And I heard nor sigh nor groan),
With heavy thump, a lifeless lump,
They dropp'd down one by one.

But Life-in-Death begins her work on the ancient Mariner.

The souls did from their bodies fly--

They fled to bliss or woe!
And every soul, it pass'd me by
Like the whizz of my crossbow!'

PART IV

The Wedding-Guest feareth that a spirit is talking to him;

'I fear thee, ancient Mariner!
I fear thy skinny hand!
And thou art long, and lank, and brown,
As is the ribb'd sea-sand.

I fear thee and thy glittering eye,
And thy skinny hand so brown.'--
'Fear not, fear not, thou Wedding-Guest!
This body dropt not down.

But the ancient Mariner assureth him of his bodily life, and proceedeth to relate his horrible penance.

Alone, alone, all, all alone,
Alone on a wide, wide sea!
And never a saint took pity on
My soul in agony.

He despiseth the creatures of the calm.

The many men, so beautiful!
And they all dead did lie:
And a thousand thousand slimy things
Lived on; and so did I.

And envieth that they should live, and so many lie dead.

I look'd upon the rotting sea,

And drew my eyes away;
I look'd upon the rotting deck,
And there the dead men lay.

I look'd to heaven, and tried to pray;
But or ever a prayer had gusht,
A wicked whisper came, and made
My heart as dry as dust.

I closed my lids, and kept them close,
And the balls like pulses beat;
For the sky and the sea, and the sea and the sky,
Lay like a load on my weary eye,
And the dead were at my feet.

But the curse liveth for him in the eye of the dead men.

The cold sweat melted from their limbs,
Nor rot nor reek did they:
The look with which they look'd on me
Had never pass'd away.

An orphan's curse would drag to hell
A spirit from on high;
But oh! more horrible than that
Is the curse in a dead man's eye!
Seven days, seven nights, I saw that curse,
And yet I could not die.

In his loneliness and fixedness he yearneth towards the journeying Moon, and the stars that still sojourn, yet still move onward; and everywhere the blue sky belongs to them, and is their appointed rest and their native country and their own natural homes, which they enter

unannounced, as lords that are certainly expected, and yet there is a silent joy at their arrival.

The moving Moon went up the sky,
And nowhere did abide;
Softly she was going up,
And a star or two beside--

Her beams bemock'd the sultry main,
Like April hoar-frost spread;
But where the ship's huge shadow lay,
The charmed water burnt alway
A still and awful red.

By the light of the Moon he beholdeth God's creatures of the great calm.

Beyond the shadow of the ship,
I watch'd the water-snakes:
They moved in tracks of shining white,
And when they rear'd, the elfish light
Fell off in hoary flakes.

Within the shadow of the ship
I watch'd their rich attire:
Blue, glossy green, and velvet black,
They coil'd and swam; and every track
Was a flash of golden fire.

Their beauty and their happiness.

O happy living things! no tongue
Their beauty might declare:
A spring of love gush'd from my heart,
And I bless'd them unaware:
Sure my kind saint took pity on me,
And I bless'd them unaware.

He blesseth them in his heart.
The spell begins to break.

The selfsame moment I could pray;
And from my neck so free
The Albatross fell off, and sank
Like lead into the sea.

PART V

'O sleep! it is a gentle thing,
Beloved from pole to pole!
To Mary Queen the praise be given!
She sent the gentle sleep from Heaven,
That slid into my soul.

By grace of the holy Mother, the ancient Mariner is refreshed with rain.

The silly buckets on the deck,
That had so long remain'd,
I dreamt that they were fill'd with dew;
And when I awoke, it rain'd.

My lips were wet, my throat was cold,
My garments all were dank;
Sure I had drunken in my dreams,
And still my body drank.

I moved, and could not feel my limbs:
I was so light--almost
I thought that I had died in sleep,
And was a blessed ghost.

He heareth sounds and seeth strange sights and commotions in the sky and the element.

And soon I heard a roaring wind:
It did not come anear;
But with its sound it shook the sails,
That were so thin and sere.

The upper air burst into life;
And a hundred fire-flags sheen;
To and fro they were hurried about!
And to and fro, and in and out,
The wan stars danced between.

And the coming wind did roar more loud,
And the sails did sigh like sedge;
And the rain pour'd down from one black cloud;
The Moon was at its edge.

The thick black cloud was cleft, and still
The Moon was at its side;
Like waters shot from some high crag,
The lightning fell with never a jag,
A river steep and wide.

The bodies of the ship's crew are inspired, and the ship moves on;

The loud wind never reach'd the ship,
Yet now the ship moved on!
Beneath the lightning and the Moon
The dead men gave a groan.

They groan'd, they stirr'd, they all uprose,
Nor spake, nor moved their eyes;
It had been strange, even in a dream,
To have seen those dead men rise.

The helmsman steer'd, the ship moved on;

Yet never a breeze up-blew;
The mariners all 'gan work the ropes,
Where they were wont to do;
They raised their limbs like lifeless tools--
We were a ghastly crew.

The body of my brother's son
Stood by me, knee to knee:
The body and I pull'd at one rope,
But he said naught to me.'

But not by the souls of the men, nor by demons of earth or middle air, but by a blessed troop of angelic spirits, sent down by the invocation of the guardian saint.

'I fear thee, ancient Mariner!'
Be calm, thou Wedding-Guest:
'Twas not those souls that fled in pain,
Which to their corses came again,
But a troop of spirits blest:

For when it dawn'd--they dropp'd their arms,
And cluster'd round the mast;
Sweet sounds rose slowly through their mouths,
And from their bodies pass'd.

Around, around, flew each sweet sound,
Then darted to the Sun;
Slowly the sounds came back again,
Now mix'd, now one by one.

Sometimes a-dropping from the sky
I heard the skylark sing;
Sometimes all little birds that are,
How they seem'd to fill the sea and air
With their sweet jargoning!

And now 'twas like all instruments,
Now like a lonely flute;
And now it is an angel's song,
That makes the Heavens be mute.

It ceased; yet still the sails made on
A pleasant noise till noon,
A noise like of a hidden brook
In the leafy month of June,
That to the sleeping woods all night
Singeth a quiet tune.

Till noon we quietly sail'd on,
Yet never a breeze did breathe:
Slowly and smoothly went the ship,
Moved onward from beneath.

The lonesome Spirit from the South Pole carries on the ship as far as the Line, in obedience to the angelic troop, but still requireth vengeance.

Under the keel nine fathom deep,
From the land of mist and snow,
The Spirit slid: and it was he
That made the ship to go.
The sails at noon left off their tune,
And the ship stood still also.

The Sun, right up above the mast,
Had fix'd her to the ocean:
But in a minute she 'gan stir,
With a short uneasy motion--
Backwards and forwards half her length
With a short uneasy motion.

Then like a pawing horse let go,
She made a sudden bound:
It flung the blood into my head,
And I fell down in a swound.

The Polar Spirit's fellow-demons, the invisible inhabitants of the element, take part in his wrong; and two of them relate, one to the other, that penance long and heavy for the ancient Mariner hath been accorded to the Polar Spirit, who returneth southward.

How long in that same fit I lay,
I have not to declare;
But ere my living life return'd,
I heard, and in my soul discern'd
Two voices in the air.

"Is it he?" quoth one, "is this the man?
By Him who died on cross,
With his cruel bow he laid full low
The harmless Albatross.

The Spirit who bideth by himself
In the land of mist and snow,
He loved the bird that loved the man
Who shot him with his bow."

The other was a softer voice,
As soft as honey-dew:
Quoth he, "The man hath penance done,
And penance more will do."

PART VI

First Voice: "'But tell me, tell me! speak again,
Thy soft response renewing--
What makes that ship drive on so fast?

What is the Ocean doing?"

Second Voice: "Still as a slave before his lord,
The Ocean hath no blast;
His great bright eye most silently
Up to the Moon is cast--

If he may know which way to go;
For she guides him smooth or grim.
See, brother, see! how graciously
She looketh down on him."

The Mariner hath been cast into a trance; for the angelic power causeth the vessel to drive northward faster than human life could endure.

First Voice: "But why drives on that ship so fast,
Without or wave or wind?"

Second Voice: "The air is cut away before,
And closes from behind.

Fly, brother, fly! more high, more high!
Or we shall be belated:
For slow and slow that ship will go,
When the Mariner's trance is abated.'

The supernatural motion is retarded; the Mariner awakes, and his penance begins anew.

I woke, and we were sailing on
As in a gentle weather:
'Twas night, calm night, the Moon was high;
The dead men stood together.

All stood together on the deck,

For a charnel-dungeon fitter:
All fix'd on me their stony eyes,
That in the Moon did glitter.

The pang, the curse, with which they died,
Had never pass'd away:
I could not draw my eyes from theirs,
Nor turn them up to pray.

The curse is finally expiated.

And now this spell was snapt: once more
I viewed the ocean green,
And look'd far forth, yet little saw
Of what had else been seen--

Like one that on a lonesome road
Doth walk in fear and dread,
And having once turn'd round, walks on,
And turns no more his head;
Because he knows a frightful fiend
Doth close behind him tread.

But soon there breathed a wind on me,
Nor sound nor motion made:
Its path was not upon the sea,
In ripple or in shade.

It raised my hair, it fann'd my cheek
Like a meadow-gale of spring--
It mingled strangely with my fears,
Yet it felt like a welcoming.

Swiftly, swiftly flew the ship,
Yet she sail'd softly too:
Sweetly, sweetly blew the breeze--

On me alone it blew.

And the ancient Mariner beholdeth his native country.

O dream of joy! is this indeed
The lighthouse top I see?
Is this the hill? is this the kirk?
Is this mine own countree?

We drifted o'er the harbour-bar,
And I with sobs did pray--
O let me be awake, my God!
Or let me sleep alway.

The harbour-bay was clear as glass,
So smoothly it was strewn!
And on the bay the moonlight lay,
And the shadow of the Moon.

The rock shone bright, the kirk no less
That stands above the rock:
The moonlight steep'd in silentness
The steady weathercock.

The angelic spirits leave the dead bodies,

And the bay was white with silent light
Till rising from the same,
Full many shapes, that shadows were,
In crimson colours came.

And appear in their own forms of light.

A little distance from the prow
Those crimson shadows were:
I turn'd my eyes upon the deck--

O Christ! what saw I there!

Each corse lay flat, lifeless and flat,
And, by the holy rood!
A man all light, a seraph-man,
On every corse there stood.

This seraph-band, each waved his hand:
It was a heavenly sight!
They stood as signals to the land,
Each one a lovely light;

This seraph-band, each waved his hand,
No voice did they impart--
No voice; but O, the silence sank
Like music on my heart.

But soon I heard the dash of oars,
I heard the Pilot's cheer;
My head was turn'd perforce away,
And I saw a boat appear.

The Pilot and the Pilot's boy,
I heard them coming fast:
Dear Lord in Heaven! it was a joy
The dead men could not blast.

I saw a third--I heard his voice:
It is the Hermit good!
He singeth loud his godly hymns
That he makes in the wood.
He'll shrieve my soul, he'll wash away
The Albatross's blood.

PART VII

The Hermit of the Wood.

'This Hermit good lives in that wood
Which slopes down to the sea.
How loudly his sweet voice he rears!
He loves to talk with marineres
That come from a far countree.

He kneels at morn, and noon, and eve--
He hath a cushion plump:
It is the moss that wholly hides
The rotted old oak-stump.

The skiff-boat near'd: I heard them talk,
"Why, this is strange, I trow!
Where are those lights so many and fair,
That signal made but now?"

Approacheth the ship with wonder.

"Strange, by my faith!" the Hermit said--
"And they answer'd not our cheer!
The planks looked warp'd! and see those sails,
How thin they are and sere!
I never saw aught like to them,
Unless perchance it were

Brown skeletons of leaves that lag
My forest-brook along;
When the ivy-tod is heavy with snow,
And the owlet whoops to the wolf below,
That eats the she-wolf's young."

"Dear Lord! it hath a fiendish look--
(The Pilot made reply)
I am a-fear'd"--"Push on, push on!"
Said the Hermit cheerily.

The boat came closer to the ship,
But I nor spake nor stirr'd;
The boat came close beneath the ship,
And straight a sound was heard.

The ship suddenly sinketh.

Under the water it rumbled on,
Still louder and more dread:
It reach'd the ship, it split the bay;
The ship went down like lead.

The ancient Mariner is saved in the Pilot's boat.

Stunn'd by that loud and dreadful sound,
Which sky and ocean smote,
Like one that hath been seven days drown'd
My body lay afloat;
But swift as dreams, myself I found
Within the Pilot's boat.

Upon the whirl, where sank the ship,
The boat spun round and round;
And all was still, save that the hill
Was telling of the sound.

I moved my lips--the Pilot shriek'd
And fell down in a fit;
The holy Hermit raised his eyes,
And pray'd where he did sit.

I took the oars: the Pilot's boy,
Who now doth crazy go,
Laugh'd loud and long, and all the while
His eyes went to and fro.
"Ha! ha!" quoth he, "full plain I see
The Devil knows how to row."

And now, all in my own countree,
I stood on the firm land!
The Hermit stepp'd forth from the boat,
And scarcely he could stand.

The ancient Mariner earnestly entreateth the Hermit to shrieve him; and the penance of life falls on him.

"O shrieve me, shrieve me, holy man!"
The Hermit cross'd his brow.
"Say quick," quoth he, "I bid thee say--
What manner of man art thou?"

Forthwith this frame of mine was wrench'd
With a woful agony,
Which forced me to begin my tale;
And then it left me free.

And ever and anon throughout his future life an agony constraineth him to travel from land to land;

Since then, at an uncertain hour,
That agony returns:
And till my ghastly tale is told,
This heart within me burns.

I pass, like night, from land to land;
I have strange power of speech;

That moment that his face I see,
I know the man that must hear me:
To him my tale I teach.

What loud uproar bursts from that door!
The wedding-guests are there:
But in the garden-bower the bride
And bride-maids singing are:
And hark the little vesper bell,
Which biddeth me to prayer!

O Wedding-Guest! this soul hath been
Alone on a wide, wide sea:
So lonely 'twas, that God Himself
Scarce seemed there to be.

O sweeter than the marriage-feast,
'Tis sweeter far to me,
To walk together to the kirk
With a goodly company!--

To walk together to the kirk,
And all together pray,
While each to his great Father bends,
Old men, and babes, and loving friends,
And youths and maidens gay!

And to teach, by his own example, love and reverence to all things that God made and loveth.

Farewell, farewell! but this I tell
To thee, thou Wedding-Guest!
He prayeth well, who loveth well
Both man and bird and beast.

He prayeth best, who loveth best

All things both great and small;
For the dear God who loveth us,
He made and loveth all.'

The Mariner, whose eye is bright,
Whose beard with age is hoar,
Is gone: and now the Wedding-Guest
Turn'd from the bridegroom's door.

He went like one that hath been stunn'd,
And is of sense forlorn:
A sadder and a wiser man
He rose the morrow morn.

A Creed

By Edwin Markham

There is a destiny that makes us brothers;
None goes his way alone:
All that we send into the lives of others
Comes back into our own.

I care not what his temples or his creeds,
One thing holds form and fast--
That into his fateful heap of days and deeds
The soul of man is cast.

The Path that Leads to Nowhere

By Corinne Roosevelt Robinson

There's a path that leads to Nowhere
In a meadow that I know,
Where an inland island rises
And the stream is still and slow;
There it wanders under willows
And beneath the silver green
Of the birches' silent shadows
Where the early violets lean.

Other pathways lead to Somewhere,
But the one I love so well
Had no end and no beginning—
Just the beauty of the dell,
Just the windflowers and the lilies
Yellow striped as adder's tongue,
Seem to satisfy my pathway
As it winds their sweets among.

There I go to meet the Springtime,
When the meadow is aglow,
Marigolds amid the marshes,—
And the stream is still and slow.—

There I find my fair oasis,
And with care-free feet I tread
For the pathway leads to Nowhere,
And the blue is overhead!

All the ways that lead to Somewhere
Echo with the hurrying feet
Of the Struggling and the Striving,
But the way I find so sweet
Bids me dream and bids me linger,
Joy and Beauty are its goal,—
On the path that leads to Nowhere
I have sometimes found my soul!

A Happy Life

By Sir Henry Wotton

How happy is he born and taught
  That serveth not another's will;
Whose armour is his honest thought,
  And simple truth his utmost skill!

Whose passions not his master's are,
  Whose soul is still prepared for death,
Not tied unto the world with care
  Of public fame, or private breath.

Youth and Age

By Samuel Taylor Coleridge

Verse, a breeze 'mid blossoms straying,
Where Hope clung feeding, like a bee--
Both were mine! Life went a-maying
With Nature, Hope, and Poesy,
        When I was young!
When I was young?--Ah, woful When!
Ah! for the change 'twixt Now and Then!
This breathing house not built with hands,
This body that does me grievous wrong,
O'er aery cliffs and glittering sands,
How lightly then it flash'd along--
Like those trim skiffs, unknown of yore,
On winding lakes and rivers wide,
That ask no aid of sail or oar,
That fear no spite of wind or tide!
Naught cared this body for wind or weather
When Youth and I lived in 't together.

Flowers are lovely! Love is flower-like;
Friendship is a sheltering tree;
O the joys, that came down shower-like,
Of Friendship, Love, and Liberty,
        Ere I was old!
Ere I was old? Ah, woful Ere,
Which tells me, Youth 's no longer here!
O Youth! for years so many and sweet,
'Tis known that thou and I were one;
I'll think it but a fond conceit--
It cannot be that thou art gone!
Thy vesper-bell hath not yet toll'd--
And thou wert aye a masker bold!

What strange disguise hast now put on,
To make believe that thou art gone?
I see these locks in silvery slips,
This drooping gait, this alter'd size:
But springtide blossoms on thy lips,
And tears take sunshine from thine eyes!
Life is but thought: so think I will
That Youth and I are housemates still.

Dewdrops are the gems of morning,
But the tears of mournful eve!
Where no hope is, life 's a warning
That only serves to make us grieve,
        When we are old!
That only serves to make us grieve
With oft and tedious taking-leave,
Like some poor nigh-related guest
That may not rudely be dismist.
Yet hath outstay'd his welcome while,
And tells the jest without the smile.

Stopping by Woods on a Snowy Evening

By Robert Frost

Whose woods these are I think I know.
His house is in the village, though;
He will not see me stopping here
To watch his woods fill up with snow.

My little horse must think it queer
To stop without a farmhouse near
Between the woods and frozen lake

The darkest evening of the year.

He gives his harness bells a shake
To ask if there is some mistake.
The only other sound's the sweep
Of easy wind and downy flake.
The woods are lovely, dark, and deep,
But I have promises to keep,
And miles to go before I sleep,
And miles to go before I sleep.

Birches

By Robert Frost

When I see birches bend to left and right
Across the lines of straighter darker trees,
I like to think some boy's been swinging them.
But swinging doesn't bend them down to stay.
Ice-storms do that. Often you must have seen them
Loaded with ice a sunny winter morning
After a rain. They click upon themselves
As the breeze rises, and turn many-coloured
As the stir cracks and crazes their enamel.

Soon the sun's warmth makes them shed crystal shells
Shattering and avalanching on the snow-crust
Such heaps of broken glass to sweep away
You'd think the inner dome of heaven had fallen.
They are dragged to the withered bracken by the load,
And they seem not to break; though once they are bowed
So low for long, they never right themselves:
You may see their trunks arching in the woods

Years afterwards, trailing their leaves on the ground,
Like girls on hands and knees that throw their hair
Before them over their heads to dry in the sun.

But I was going to say when Truth broke in
With all her matter-of-fact about the ice-storm,
I should prefer to have some boy bend them
As he went out and in to fetch the cows--
Some boy too far from town to learn baseball,
Whose only play was what he found himself,
Summer or winter, and could play alone.

One by one he subdued his father's trees
By riding them down over and over again
Until he took the stiffness out of them,
And not one but hung limp, not one was left
For him to conquer. He learned all there was
To learn about not launching out too soon
And so not carrying the tree away
Clear to the ground. He always kept his poise
To the top branches, climbing carefully
With the same pains you use to fill a cup
Up to the brim, and even above the brim.

Then he flung outward, feet first, with a swish,
Kicking his way down through the air to the ground.
So was I once myself a swinger of birches.
And so I dream of going back to be.
It's when I'm weary of considerations,
And life is too much like a pathless wood
Where your face burns and tickles with the cobwebs
Broken across it, and one eye is weeping
From a twig's having lashed across it open.

I'd like to get away from earth awhile
And then come back to it and begin over.
May no fate willfully misunderstand me

And half grant what I wish and snatch me away
Not to return. Earth's the right place for love:
I don't know where it's likely to go better.

I'd like to go by climbing a birch tree
And climb black branches up a snow-white trunk
Toward heaven, till the tree could bear no more,
But dipped its top and set me down again.
That would be good both going and coming back.
One could do worse than be a swinger of birches.

The Ballad of the Northern Lights

By Robert William Service

One of the Down and Out--that's me. Stare at me well, ay, stare!

Stare and shrink--say! you wouldn't think that I was a millionaire.

Look at my face, it's crimped and gouged--one of them death-mask things;

Don't seem the sort of man, do I, as might be the pal of kings?

Slouching along in smelly rags, a bleary-eyed, no-good bum;

A knight of the hollow needle, pard, spewed from the sodden slum.

Look me all over from head to foot; how much would you think I was worth?

A dollar? a dime? a nickel? Why, I'm the wealthest man on earth.

No, don't you think that I'm off my base. You'll sing a different tune

If only you'll let me spin my yarn. Come over to this saloon;

Wet my throat--it's as dry as chalk, and seeing as how it's you,

I'll tell the tale of a Northern trail, and so help me God, it's true.

I'll tell of the howling wilderness and the haggard Arctic heights,

Of a reckless vow that I made, and how I staked the Northern Lights.

Remember the year of the Big Stampede and the trail of Ninety-eight,

When the eyes of the world were turned to the North, and the hearts of men elate;

Hearts of the old dare-devil breed thrilled at the wondrous strike,

And to every man who could hold a pan came the message, "Up and hike".

Well, I was there with the best of them, and I knew I would not fail.

You wouldn't believe it to see me now; but wait till you've heard my tale.

You've read of the trail of Ninety-eight, but its woe no man may tell;

It was all of a piece and a whole yard wide, and the name of the brand was "Hell".

We heard the call and we staked our all; we were plungers playing blind,

And no man cared how his neighbor fared, and no man looked behind;

For a ruthless greed was born of need, and the weakling went to the wall,

And a curse might avail where a prayer would fail, and the gold lust crazed us all.

Bold were we, and they called us three the "Unholy Trinity";

There was Ole Olson, the Sailor Swede, and the Dago Kid and me.

We were the discards of the pack, the foreloopers of Unrest,

Reckless spirits of fierce revolt in the ferment of the West.

We were bound to win and we revelled in the hardships of the way.

We staked our ground and our hopes were crowned, and we hoisted out the pay.

We were rich in a day beyond our dreams, it was gold from the grass-roots down;

But we weren't used to such sudden wealth, and there was the siren town.

We were crude and careless frontiersmen, with much in us of the beast;

We could bear the famine worthily, but we lost our heads at the feast.

The town looked mighty bright to us, with a bunch of dust to spend,

And nothing was half too good them days, and everyone was our friend.

Wining meant more than mining then, and life was a dizzy whirl,

Gambling and dropping chunks of gold down the neck of a dance-hall girl;
Till we went clean mad, it seems to me, and we squandered our last poke,
And we sold our claim, and we found ourselves one bitter morning--broke.

The Dago Kid he dreamed a dream of his mother's aunt who died--
In the dawn-light dim she came to him, and she stood by his bedside,
And she said: "Go forth to the highest North till a lonely trail ye find;
Follow it far and trust your star, and fortune will be kind."
But I jeered at him, and then there came the Sailor Swede to me,
And he said: "I dreamed of my sister's son, who croaked at the age of three.
From the herded dead he sneaked and said: `Seek you an Arctic trail;
'Tis pale and grim by the Polar rim, but seek and ye shall not fail.'"
And lo! that night I too did dream of my mother's sister's son,
And he said to me: "By the Arctic Sea there's a treasure to be won.
Follow and follow a lone moose trail, till you come to a valley grim,
On the slope of the lonely watershed that borders the Polar brim."

Then I woke my pals, and soft we swore by the mystic Silver Flail,

'Twas the hand of Fate, and to-morrow straight we would seek the lone moose trail.

We watched the groaning ice wrench free, crash on with a hollow din;

Men of the wilderness were we, freed from the taint of sin.

The mighty river snatched us up and it bore us swift along;

The days were bright, and the morning light was sweet with jewelled song.

We poled and lined up nameless streams, portaged o'er hill and plain;

We burnt our boat to save the nails, and built our boat again;

We guessed and groped, North, ever North, with many a twist and turn;

We saw ablaze in the deathless days the splendid sunsets burn.

O'er soundless lakes where the grayling makes a rush at the clumsy fly;

By bluffs so steep that the hard-hit sheep falls sheer from out the sky;

By lilied pools where the bull moose cools and wallows in huge content;

By rocky lairs where the pig-eyed bears peered at our tiny tent.

Through the black canyon's angry foam we hurled to dreamy bars,

And round in a ring the dog-nosed peaks bayed to the mocking stars.

Spring and summer and autumn went; the sky had a tallow gleam,
Yet North and ever North we pressed to the land of our Golden Dream.

So we came at last to a tundra vast and dark and grim and lone;
And there was the little lone moose trail, and we knew it for our own.
By muskeg hollow and nigger-head it wandered endlessly;
Sorry of heart and sore of foot, weary men were we.
The short-lived sun had a leaden glare and the darkness came too soon,
And stationed there with a solemn stare was the pinched, anaemic moon.
Silence and silvern solitude till it made you dumbly shrink,
And you thought to hear with an outward ear the things you thought to think.

Oh, it was wild and weird and wan, and ever in camp o' nights
We would watch and watch the silver dance of the mystic Northern Lights.
And soft they danced from the Polar sky and swept in primrose haze;
And swift they pranced with their silver feet, and pierced with a blinding blaze.
They danced a cotillion in the sky; they were rose and silver shod;
It was not good for the eyes of man--'twas a sight for the eyes of God.

It made us mad and strange and sad, and the gold whereof we dreamed
Was all forgot, and our only thought was of the lights that gleamed.

Oh, the tundra sponge it was golden brown, and some was a bright blood-red;
And the reindeer moss gleamed here and there like the tombstones of the dead.
And in and out and around about the little trail ran clear,
And we hated it with a deadly hate and we feared with a deadly fear.
And the skies of night were alive with light, with a throbbing, thrilling flame;
Amber and rose and violet, opal and gold it came.
It swept the sky like a giant scythe, it quivered back to a wedge;
Argently bright, it cleft the night with a wavy golden edge.
Pennants of silver waved and streamed, lazy banners unfurled;
Sudden splendors of sabres gleamed, lightning javelins were hurled.
There in our awe we crouched and saw with our wild, uplifted eyes
Charge and retire the hosts of fire in the battlefield of the skies.

But all things come to an end at last, and the muskeg melted away,
And frowning down to bar our path a muddle of mountains lay.

And a gorge sheered up in granite walls, and the moose trail crept betwixt;

'Twas as if the earth had gaped too far and her stony jaws were fixt.

Then the winter fell with a sudden swoop, and the heavy clouds sagged low,

And earth and sky were blotted out in a whirl of driving snow.

We were climbing up a glacier in the neck of a mountain pass,

When the Dago Kid slipped down and fell into a deep crevasse.

When we got him out one leg hung limp, and his brow was wreathed with pain,

And he says: "'Tis badly broken, boys, and I'll never walk again.

It's death for all if ye linger here, and that's no cursed lie;

Go on, go on while the trail is good, and leave me down to die."

He raved and swore, but we tended him with our uncouth, clumsy care.

The camp-fire gleamed and he gazed and dreamed with a fixed and curious stare.

Then all at once he grabbed my gun and he put it to his head,

And he says: "I'll fix it for you, boys"--them are the words he said.

So we sewed him up in a canvas sack and we slung him to a tree;

And the stars like needles stabbed our eyes, and woeful men were we.

And on we went on our woeful way, wrapped in a daze of dream,

And the Northern Lights in the crystal nights came forth with a mystic gleam.

They danced and they danced the devil-dance over the naked snow;

And soft they rolled like a tide upshoaled with a ceaseless ebb and flow.

They rippled green with a wondrous sheen, they fluttered out like a fan;

They spread with a blaze of rose-pink rays never yet seen of man.

They writhed like a brood of angry snakes, hissing and sulphur pale;

Then swift they changed to a dragon vast, lashing a cloven tail.

It seemed to us, as we gazed aloft with an everlasting stare,

The sky was a pit of bale and dread, and a monster revelled there.

We climbed the rise of a hog-back range that was desolate and drear,

When the Sailor Swede had a crazy fit, and he got to talking queer.

He talked of his home in Oregon and the peach trees all in bloom,

And the fern head-high, and the topaz sky, and the forest's scented gloom.

He talked of the sins of his misspent life, and then he seemed to brood,

And I watched him there like a fox a hare, for I knew it was not good.

And sure enough in the dim dawn-light I missed him from the tent,

And a fresh trail broke through the crusted snow, and I knew not where it went.

But I followed it o'er the seamless waste, and I found him at shut of day,

Naked there as a new-born babe--so I left him where he lay.

Day after day was sinister, and I fought fierce-eyed despair,

And I clung to life, and I struggled on, I knew not why nor where.

I packed my grub in short relays, and I cowered down in my tent,

And the world around was purged of sound like a frozen continent.

Day after day was dark as death, but ever and ever at nights,

With a brilliancy that grew and grew, blazed up the Northern Lights.

They rolled around with a soundless sound like softly bruised silk;

They poured into the bowl of the sky with the gentle flow of milk.

In eager, pulsing violet their wheeling chariots came,

Or they poised above the Polar rim like a coronal of flame.

From depths of darkness fathomless their lancing rays were hurled,

Like the all-combining search-lights of the navies of the world.

There on the roof-pole of the world as one bewitched I gazed,

And howled and grovelled like a beast as the awful splendors blazed.

My eyes were seared, yet thralled I peered through the parka hood nigh blind;

But I staggered on to the lights that shone, and never I looked behind.

There is a mountain round and low that lies by the Polar rim,

And I climbed its height in a whirl of light, and I peered o'er its jagged brim;

And there in a crater deep and vast, ungained, unguessed of men,

The mystery of the Arctic world was flashed into my ken.

For there these poor dim eyes of mine beheld the sight of sights--

That hollow ring was the source and spring of the mystic Northern Lights.

Then I staked that place from crown to base, and I hit the homeward trail.

Ah, God! it was good, though my eyes were blurred, and I crawled like a sickly snail.

In that vast white world where the silent sky communes with the silent snow,

In hunger and cold and misery I wandered to and fro.

But the Lord took pity on my pain, and He led me to the sea,

And some ice-bound whalers heard my moan, and they fed and sheltered me.

They fed the feeble scarecrow thing that stumbled out of the wild
With the ravaged face of a mask of death and the wandering wits of a child--
A craven, cowering bag of bones that once had been a man.
They tended me and they brought me back to the world, and here I am.

Some say that the Northern Lights are the glare of the Arctic ice and snow;
And some that it's electricity, and nobody seems to know.
But I'll tell you now--and if I lie, may my lips be stricken dumb--
It's a mine, a mine of the precious stuff that men call radium.
It's a million dollars a pound, they say, and there's tons and tons in sight.
You can see it gleam in a golden stream in the solitudes of night.
And it's mine, all mine--and say! if you have a hundred plunks to spare,
I'll let you have the chance of your life, I'll sell you a quarter share.
You turn it down? Well, I'll make it ten, seeing as you are my friend.
Nothing doing? Say! don't be hard--have you got a dollar to lend?
Just a dollar to help me out, I know you'll treat me white;
I'll do as much for you some day . . . God bless you, sir; good-night.

The Road Not Taken

By Robert Frost

Two roads diverged in a yellow wood,
And sorry I could not travel both
And be one traveler, long I stood
And looked down one as far as I could
To where it bent in the undergrowth.

Then took the other, as just as fair,
And having perhaps the better claim,
Because it was grassy and wanted wear;
Though as for that the passing there
Had worn them really about the same.

And both that morning equally lay
In leaves no step had trodden black.
Oh, I kept the first for another day!
Yet knowing how way leads on to way,
I doubted if I should ever come back.

I shall be telling this with a sigh
Somewhere ages and ages hence:
Two roads diverged in a wood, and I--
I took the one less traveled by,
And that has made all the difference.

Woodman, Spare That Tree

By George Pope Morris

Woodman, spare that tree!
Touch not a single bough!
In youth it sheltered me,
And I'll protect it now.
'Twas my forefather's hand
That placed it near his cot;
There, woodman, let it stand,
Thy axe shall harm it not!
That old familiar tree,
Whose glory and renown
Are spread o'er land and sea,
And wouldst thou hew it down?
Woodman, forbear thy stroke!
Cut not its earth-bound ties;
O, spare that aged oak,
Now towering to the skies!
When but an idle boy
I sought its grateful shade;
In all their gushing joy
Here too my sisters played.
My mother kissed me here;
My father pressed my hand --
Forgive this foolish tear,
But let that old oak stand!
My heart-strings round thee cling,
Close as thy bark, old friend!
Here shall the wild-bird sing,
And still thy branches bend.
Old tree! the storm still brave!

And, woodman, leave the spot;
While I've a hand to save,
Thy axe shall hurt it not.

Along the Road

By Robert Browning Hamilton

I walked a mile with Pleasure,
She chattered all the way;
But left me none the wiser,
For all she had to say.
I walked a mile with Sorrow
And ne'er a word said she;
But, oh, the things I learned from her
When Sorrow walked with me!

Lying In A Hammock At William Duffy's Farm In Pine Island, Minnesota

By James Wright

Over my head, I see the bronze butterfly,
Asleep on the black trunk,
blowing like a leaf in green shadow.
Down the ravine behind the empty house,
The cowbells follow one another
Into the distances of the afternoon.
To my right,
In a field of sunlight between two pines,
The droppings of last year's horses
Blaze up into golden stones.
I lean back, as the evening darkens and comes on.
A chicken hawk floats over, looking for home.
I have wasted my life.

After Apple-Picking

By Robert Frost

My long two-pointed ladder's sticking through a tree
Toward heaven still,
And there's a barrel that I didn't fill
Beside it, and there may be two or three
Apples I didn't pick upon some bough.
But I am done with apple-picking now.
Essence of winter sleep is on the night,
The scent of apples: I am drowsing off.
I cannot rub the strangeness from my sight
I got from looking through a pane of glass
I skimmed this morning from the drinking trough
And held against the world of hoary grass.
It melted, and I let it fall and break.
But I was well
Upon my way to sleep before it fell,
And I could tell
What form my dreaming was about to take.
Magnified apples appear and disappear,
Stem end and blossom end,
And every fleck of russet showing clear.
My instep arch not only keeps the ache,
It keeps the pressure of a ladder-round.
I feel the ladder sway as the boughs bend.

And I keep hearing from the cellar bin
The rumbling sound
Of load on load of apples coming in.
For I have had too much
Of apple-picking: I am overtired
Of the great harvest I myself desired.
There were ten thousand thousand fruit to touch,
Cherish in hand, lift down, and not let fall.

For all
That struck the earth,
No matter if not bruised or spiked with stubble,
Went surely to the cider-apple heap
As of no worth.
One can see what will trouble
This sleep of mine, whatever sleep it is.
Were he not gone,
The woodchuck could say whether it's like his
Long sleep, as I describe its coming on,
Or just some human sleep.

If

By Rudyard Kipling

If you can keep your head when all about you
Are losing theirs and blaming it on you,
If you can trust yourself when all men doubt you
But make allowance for their doubting too,
If you can wait and not be tired by waiting,
Or being lied about, don't deal in lies,
Or being hated, don't give way to hating,
And yet don't look too good, nor talk too wise:

If you can dream--and not make dreams your master,
If you can think--and not make thoughts your aim;
If you can meet with Triumph and Disaster
And treat those two impostors just the same;
If you can bear to hear the truth you've spoken
Twisted by knaves to make a trap for fools,
Or watch the things you gave your life to, broken,
And stoop and build 'em up with worn-out tools:

If you can make one heap of all your winnings
And risk it all on one turn of pitch-and-toss,
And lose, and start again at your beginnings
And never breath a word about your loss;
If you can force your heart and nerve and sinew
To serve your turn long after they are gone,
And so hold on when there is nothing in you
Except the Will which says to them: "Hold on!"

If you can talk with crowds and keep your virtue,
Or walk with kings--nor lose the common touch,
If neither foes nor loving friends can hurt you;
If all men count with you, but none too much,
If you can fill the unforgiving minute
With sixty seconds' worth of distance run,
Yours is the Earth and everything that's in it,
And--which is more--you'll be a Man, my son!

The Negro Speaks of Rivers

By Langston Hughes

I've known rivers:
I've known rivers ancient as the world and older than the flow
of human blood in human veins.
My soul has grown deep like the rivers.

I bathed in the Euphrates when dawns were young.
I built my hut near the Congo and it lulled me to sleep.

I looked upon the Nile and raised the pyramids above it.
I heard the singing of the Mississippi when Abe Lincoln went
down to New Orleans, and I've seen its muddy bosom
turn all golden in the sunset.

I've known rivers:
Ancient, dusky rivers.

My soul has grown deep like the rivers.

Far From the Madding Crowd

By Nixon Waterman

It seems to me I'd like to go
Where bells don't ring, nor whistles blow,
Nor clocks don't strike, nor gongs sound,
And I'd have stillness all around.

Not real stillness, but just the trees,
Low whispering, or the hum of bees,
Or brooks faint babbling over stones,
In strangely, softly tangled tones.

Or maybe a cricket or katydid,
Or the songs of birds in the hedges hid,
Or just some sweet sounds as these,
To fill a tired heart with ease.

If 'tweren't for sight and sound and smell
I'd like the city pretty well,
But when it comes to getting rest,
I like the country lots the best.

Sometimes it seems to me I must
Just quit the city's din and dust,
And get out where the sky is blue,
And say, now, how does it seem to you?

The Chambered Nautilus

By Oliver Wendell Holmes

This is the ship of pearl, which, poets feign,
Sail the unshadowed main,--
The venturous bark that flings
On the sweet summer wind its purpled wings
In gulfs enchanted, where the Siren sings,
And coral reefs lie bare,
Where the cold sea-maids rise to sun their streaming hair.

Its webs of living gauze no more unfurl;
Wrecked is the ship of pearl!
And every chambered cell,
Where its dim dreaming life was wont to dwell,
As the frail tenant shaped his growing shell,
Before thee lies revealed,--
Its irised ceiling rent, its sunless crypt unsealed!

Year after year beheld the silent toil
That spread his lustrous coil;
Still, as the spiral grew,
He left the past year's dwelling for the new,
Stole with soft step its shining archway through,
Built up its idle door,
Stretched in his last-found home, and knew the old no more.

Thanks for the heavenly message brought by thee,
Child of the wandering sea,
Cast from her lap, forlorn!
From thy dead lips a clearer note is born
Than ever Triton blew from wreathed horn;
While on mine ear it rings,
Through the deep caves of thought I hear a voice that sings:--

Build thee more stately mansions, O my soul,
As the swift seasons roll!
Leave thy low-vaulted past!
Let each new temple, nobler than the last,
Shut thee from heaven with a dome more vast,
Till thou at length art free,
Leaving thine outgrown shell by life's unresting sea!

The Bird with the Coppery, Keen Claws

By Wallace Stevens

Above the forest of the parakeets,
A parakeet of parakeets prevails,
A pip of life amid a mort of tails.

(The rudiments of tropics are around,
Aloe of ivory, pear of rusty rind.)
His lids are white because his eyes are blind.

He is not paradise of parakeets,
Of his gold ether, golden alguazil,
Except because he broods there and is still.

Panache upon panache, his tails deploy
Upward and outward, in green-vented forms,
His tip a drop of water full of storms.

But though the turbulent tinges undulate
As his pure intellect applies its laws,
He moves not on his coppery, keen claws.

He munches a dry shell while he exerts
His will, yet never ceases, perfect cock,
To flare, in the sun-pallor of his rock.

There Was A Child Went Forth

By Walt Whitman

There was a child went forth every day;
And the first object he look'd upon, that object he became;
And that object became part of him for the day, or a certain part of
the day, or for many years, or stretching cycles of years.

The early lilacs became part of this child,
And grass, and white and red morning-glories, and white and red clover, and the song of the phoebe-bird,
And the Third-month lambs, and the sow's pink-faint litter, and the mare's foal, and the cow's calf,
And the noisy brood of the barn-yard, or by the mire of the pond-side,
And the fish suspending themselves so curiously below there--and the beautiful curious liquid,
And the water-plants with their graceful flat heads--all became part of him.

The field-sprouts of Fourth-month and Fifth-month became part of him;
Winter-grain sprouts, and those of the light-yellow corn, and the esculent roots of the garden,
And the apple-trees cover'd with blossoms, and the fruit afterward,
and wood-berries, and the commonest weeds by the road;
And the old drunkard staggering home from the out-house of the tavern, whence he had lately risen,
And the school-mistress that pass'd on her way to the school,
And the friendly boys that pass'd--and the quarrelsome boys,
And the tidy and fresh-cheek'd girls--and the barefoot negro boy and girl,

And all the changes of city and country, wherever he went.

His own parents,
He that had father'd him, and she that had conceiv'd him in
her womb, and birth'd him,
They gave this child more of themselves than that;
They gave him afterward every day--they became part of him.

The mother at home, quietly placing the dishes on the supper-
table;
The mother with mild words--clean her cap and gown, a
wholesome odor
falling off her person and clothes as she walks by;
The father, strong, self-sufficient, manly, mean, anger'd,
unjust;
The blow, the quick loud word, the tight bargain, the crafty
lure,
The family usages, the language, the company, the furniture--
the yearning and swelling heart,
Affection that will not be gainsay'd--the sense of what is real--
the thought if, after all, it should prove unreal,
The doubts of day-time and the doubts of night-time--the
curious whether and how,
Whether that which appears so is so, or is it all flashes and
specks?
Men and women crowding fast in the streets--if they are not
flashes and specks, what are they?
The streets themselves, and the façades of houses, and
goods in the windows,
Vehicles, teams, the heavy-plank'd wharves--the huge crossing
at the ferries,
The village on the highland, seen from afar at sunset--the river
between,
Shadows, aureola and mist, the light falling on roofs and
gables of white or brown, three miles off,
The schooner near by, sleepily dropping down the tide--the

little boat slack-tow'd astern,
The hurrying tumbling waves, quick-broken crests, slapping,
The strata of color'd clouds, the long bar of maroon-tint, away solitary by itself--the spread of purity it lies motionless in,
The horizon's edge, the flying sea-crow, the fragrance of salt marsh and shore mud;
These became part of that child who went forth every day, and who now goes, and will always go forth every day.

Leisure

By William Henry Davies

What is this life if, full of care,
We have no time to stand and stare.

No time to stand beneath the boughs
And stare as long as sheep or cows.

No time to see, when woods we pass,
Where squirrels hide their nuts in grass.

No time to see, in broad daylight,
Streams full of stars, like skies at night.

No time to turn at Beauty's glance,
And watch her feet, how they can dance.

No time to wait till her mouth can
Enrich that smile her eyes began.

A poor life this if, full of care,
We have no time to stand and stare.

My Heart Leaps Up

By William Wordsworth

My heart leaps up when I behold
A rainbow in the sky:
So was it when my life began,
So is it now I am a man,
So be it when I shall grow old
Or let me die!
The Child is father of the Man:
And I could wish my days to be
Bound each to each by natural piety.

I Wandered Lonely as a Cloud

By William Wordsworth

I wandered lonely as a cloud
That floats on high o'er vales and hills,
When all at once I saw a crowd,
A host, of golden daffodils;
Beside the lake, beneath the trees,
Fluttering and dancing in the breeze.

Continuous as the stars that shine
And twinkle on the milky way,
They stretched in never-ending line
Along the margin of a bay:
Ten thousand saw I at a glance,
Tossing their heads in sprightly dance.

The waves beside them danced; but they
Out-did the sparkling waves in glee:
A poet could not but be gay,
In such a jocund company:
I gazed---and gazed---but little thought
What wealth the show to me had brought:

For oft, when on my couch I lie
In vacant or in pensive mood,
They flash upon that inward eye
Which is the bliss of solitude;
And then my heart with pleasure fills,
And dances with the daffodils.

No Man is an Island

By John Donne

No man is an island entire of itself; every man
is a piece of the continent, a part of the main;
if a clod be washed away by the sea, Europe
is the less, as well as if a promontory were, as
well as any manner of thy friends or of thine
own were; any man's death diminishes me,
because I am involved in mankind.
And therefore never send to know for whom
the bell tolls; it tolls for thee.

The World's All Right

By Robert William Service

Be honest, kindly, simple, true;
Seek good in all, scorn but pretence;
Whatever sorrow come to you,
Believe in Life's Beneficence!

The World's all right; serene I sit,
And cease to puzzle over it.
There's much that's mighty strange, no doubt;
But Nature knows what she's about;
And in a million years or so
We'll know more than to-day we know.
Old Evolution's under way --
  What ho! the World's all right, I say.

Could things be other than they are?
All's in its place, from mote to star.
The thistledown that flits and flies
Could drift no hair-breadth otherwise.
What is, must be; with rhythmic laws
All Nature chimes, Effect and Cause.
The sand-grain and the sun obey --
  What ho! the World's all right, I say.

Just try to get the Cosmic touch,
The sense that "you" don't matter much.
A million stars are in the sky;
A million planets plunge and die;
A million million men are sped;
A million million wait ahead.
Each plays his part and has his day --
    What ho! the World's all right, I say.

Just try to get the Chemic view:
A million million lives made "you".
In lives a million you will be
Immortal down Eternity;
Immortal on this earth to range,
With never death, but ever change.
You always were, and will be aye --
    What ho! the World's all right, I say.

Be glad! And do not blindly grope
For Truth that lies beyond our scope:
A sober plot informeth all
Of Life's uproarious carnival.
Your day is such a little one,
A gnat that lives from sun to sun;
Yet gnat and you have parts to play --
    What ho! the World's all right, I say.

And though it's written from the start,
Just act your best your little part.
Just be as happy as you can,
And serve your kind, and die -- a man.
Just live the good that in you lies,
And seek no guerdon of the skies;
Just make your Heaven here, to-day --
    What ho! the World's all right, I say.

Remember! in Creation's swing
The Race and not the man's the thing.
There's battle, murder, sudden death,
And pestilence, with poisoned breath.
Yet quick forgotten are such woes;
On, on the stream of Being flows.
Truth, Beauty, Love uphold their sway --
    What ho! the World's all right, I say.

The World's all right; serene I sit,
And joy that I am part of it;
And put my trust in Nature's plan,
And try to aid her all I can;
Content to pass, if in my place
I've served the uplift of the Race.
Truth! Beauty! Love! O Radiant Day --
    What ho! the World's all right, I say.

Cupid Stung

By Thomas Moore

Cupid once upon a bed
Of roses laid his weary head;
Luckless urchin, not to see
Within the leaves a slumbering bee.
The bee awak'd--with anger wild
The bee awak'd, and stung the child.
Loud and piteous are his cries;
To Venus quick he runs, he flies;
"Oh, Mother! I am wounded through--
I die with pain--in sooth I do!
Stung by some little angry thing,
Some serpent on a tiny wing--
A bee it was--for once, I know,
I heard a rustic call it so."
Thus he spoke, and she the while
Heard him with a soothing smile;
Then said, "My infant, if so much
Thou feel the little wild bee's touch,
How must the heart, ah, Cupid! be,
The hapless heart that's stung by thee!"

A Vagabond Song

By Bliss Carman

There is something in the autumn that is native to my blood --
Touch of manner, hint of mood;
And my heart is like a rhyme,
With the yellow and the purple and the crimson keeping time.

The scarlet of the maples can shake me like a cry
Of bugles going by.
And my lonely spirit thrills
To see the frosty asters like a smoke upon the hills.

There is something in October sets the gypsy blood astir;
We must rise and follow her,
When from every hill of flame
She calls and calls each vagabond by name.

The Wise Old Owl

By Edward H. Richards

The wise old owl lived in an oak;
The more he saw the less he spoke;
The less he spoke the more he heard:
Why can't we all be like that bird?

Miracles

By Walt Whitman

Why, who makes much of a miracle?
As to me I know of nothing else but miracles,
Whether I walk the streets of Manhattan,
Or dart my sight over the roofs of houses toward the sky,
Or wade with naked feet along the beach just in the edge of
the water,
Or stand under trees in the woods,
Or talk by day with any one I love, or sleep in the bed at night
with any one I love,
Or sit at table at dinner with the rest,
Or look at strangers opposite me riding in the car,
Or watch honey-bees busy around the hive of a summer
forenoon,
Or animals feeding in the fields,
Or birds, or the wonderfulness of insects in the air,
Or the wonderfulness of the sundown, or of stars shining so
quiet
and bright,
Or the exquisite delicate thin curve of the new moon in spring;
These with the rest, one and all, are to me miracles,
The whole referring, yet each distinct and in its place.

To me every hour of the light and dark is a miracle,
Every cubic inch of space is a miracle,
Every square yard of the surface of the earth is spread with the
same,
Every foot of the interior swarms with the same.
To me the sea is a continual miracle,
The fishes that swim--the rocks--the motion of the waves--the
ships with men in them,
What stranger miracles are there?

The Common Road

By Silas H. Perkins

I want to travel the common road
With the great crowd surging by,
Where there's many a laugh and many a load,
And many a smile and sigh.
I want to be on the common way
With its endless tramping feet,
In the summer bright and winter gray,
In the noonday sun and heat.
In the cool of evening with shadows nigh,
At dawn, when the sun breaks clear,
I want the great crowd passing by,
To ken what they see and hear.
I want to be one of the common herd,
Not live in a sheltered way,
Want to be thrilled, want to be stirred,
By the great crowd day by day;
To glimpse the restful valleys deep,
To toil up the rugged hill,
To see the brooks which shyly creep,
To have the torrents thrill.
I want to laugh with the common man
Wherever he chance to be,
I want to aid him when I can
Whenever there's need of me.
I want to lend a helping hand
Over the rough and steep
To a child too young to understand-
To comfort those who weep.
I want to live and work and plan
With the great crowd surging by,
To mingle with the common man,
No better or worse than I.

To the Thawing Wind

By Robert Frost

Come with rain. O loud Southwester!
Bring the singer, bring the nester;
Give the buried flower a dream;
make the settled snowbank steam;
Find the brown beneath the white;
But whate'er you do tonight,
bath my window, make it flow,
Melt it as the ice will go;
Melt the glass and leave the sticks
Like a hermit's crucifix;
Burst into my narrow stall;
Swing the picture on the wall;
Run the rattling pages o'er;
Scatter poems on the floor;
Turn the poet out of door.

Alone

By Edgar Allen Poe

From childhood's hour I have not been
As others were; I have not seen
As others saw; I could not bring
My passions from a common spring.
From the same source I have not taken
My sorrow; I could not awaken
My heart to joy at the same tone;
And all I loved, I loved alone.

Then- in my childhood, in the dawn
Of a most stormy life- was drawn
From every depth of good and ill
The mystery which binds me still:
From the torrent, or the fountain,
From the red cliff of the mountain,
From the sun that round me rolled
In its autumn tint of gold,
From the lightning in the sky
As it passed me flying by,
From the thunder and the storm,
And the cloud that took the form
(When the rest of Heaven was blue)
Of a demon in my view.

Mending Wall

By Robert Frost

Something there is that doesn't love a wall,
That sends the frozen-ground-swell under it,
And spills the upper boulders in the sun;
And makes gaps even two can pass abreast.
The work of hunters is another thing:
I have come after them and made repair
Where they have left not one stone on a stone,
But they would have the rabbit out of hiding,
To please the yelping dogs. The gaps I mean,
No one has seen them made or heard them made,
But at spring mending-time we find them there.
I let my neighbor know beyond the hill;
And on a day we meet to walk the line
And set the wall between us once again.
We keep the wall between us as we go.

To each the boulders that have fallen to each.
And some are loaves and some so nearly balls
We have to use a spell to make them balance:
'Stay where you are until our backs are turned!'
We wear our fingers rough with handling them.
Oh, just another kind of outdoor game,
One on a side. It comes to little more:
There where it is we do not need the wall:
He is all pine and I am apple orchard.
My apple trees will never get across
And eat the cones under his pines, I tell him.
He only says, 'Good fences make good neighbors.'
Spring is the mischief in me, and I wonder
If I could put a notion in his head:
'*Why* do they make good neighbors? Isn't it
Where there are cows? But here there are no cows.
Before I built a wall I'd ask to know
What I was walling in or walling out,
And to whom I was like to give offense.
Something there is that doesn't love a wall,
That wants it down.' I could say 'Elves' to him,
But it's not elves exactly, and I'd rather
He said it for himself. I see him there
Bringing a stone grasped firmly by the top
In each hand, like an old-stone savage armed.
He moves in darkness as it seems to me,
Not of woods only and the shade of trees.
He will not go behind his father's saying,
And he likes having thought of it so well
He says again, 'Good fences make good neighbors.'

Conscience

By Henry David Thoreau

Conscience is instinct bred in the house,
Feeling and Thinking propagate the sin
By an unnatural breeding in and in.
I say, Turn it out doors,
Into the moors.
I love a life whose plot is simple,
And does not thicken with every pimple,
A soul so sound no sickly conscience binds it,
That makes the universe no worse than 't finds it.
I love an earnest soul,
Whose mighty joy and sorrow
Are not drowned in a bowl,
And brought to life to-morrow;
That lives one tragedy,
And not seventy;
A conscience worth keeping;
Laughing not weeping;
A conscience wise and steady,
And forever ready;
Not changing with events,
Dealing in compliments;
A conscience exercised about
Large things, where one may doubt.
I love a soul not all of wood,
Predestinated to be good,
But true to the backbone
Unto itself alone,
And false to none;
Born to its own affairs,
Its own joys and own cares;
By whom the work which God begun
Is finished, and not undone;

Taken up where he left off,
Whether to worship or to scoff;
If not good, why then evil,
If not good god, good devil.
Goodness! you hypocrite, come out of that,
Live your life, do your work, then take your hat.
I have no patience towards
Such conscientious cowards.
Give me simple laboring folk,
Who love their work,
Whose virtue is song
To cheer God along.

Delight Becomes Pictorial

By Emily Dickinson

Delight -- becomes pictorial --
When viewed through Pain --
More fair -- because impossible
Than any gain --

The Mountain -- at a given distance --
In Amber -- lies --
Approached -- the Amber flits -- a little --
And That's -- the Skies –

Song of a Man Who Has Come Through

By D.H. Lawrence

Not I, not I, but the wind that blows through me!
A fine wind is blowing the new direction of Time.
If only I let it bear me, carry me, if only it carry me!
If only I am sensitive, subtle, oh, delicate, a winged gift!
If only, most lovely of all, I yield myself and am borrowed
By the fine, fine wind that takes its course through the chaos of the world
Like a fine, an exquisite chisel, a wedge-blade inserted;
If only I am keen and hard like the sheer tip of a wedge
Driven by invisible blows,
The rock will split, we shall come at the wonder, we shall find the Hesperides.

Oh, for the wonder that bubbles into my soul,
I would be a good fountain, a good well-head,
Would blur no whisper, spoil no expression.

What is the knocking?
What is the knocking at the door in the night?
It is somebody wants to do us harm.

No, no, it is the three strange angels.
Admit them, admit them.

The Inchcape Rock

By Robert Southey

No stir in the air, no stir in the sea,
The ship was still as she could be;
Her sails from heaven received no motion;
Her keel was steady in the ocean.

Without either sign or sound of their shock,
The waves flowed over the Inchcape Rock;
So little they rose, so little they fell,
They did not move the Inchcape Bell.

The Abbot of Aberbrothok
Had placed that Bell on the Inchcape Rock;
On a buoy in the storm it floated and swung,
And over the waves its warning rung.

When the Rock was hid by the surge's swell,
The mariners heard the warning Bell;
And then they knew the perilous Rock,
And blest the Abbot of Aberbrothok.

The sun in heaven was shining gay;
All things were joyful on that day;
The sea-birds screamed as they wheeled round,
And there was joyance in their sound.

The buoy of the Inchcape Bell was seen,
A dark spot on the ocean green;
Sir Ralph the Rover walked his deck,
And he fixed his eye on the darker speck.

He felt the cheering power of spring;
It made him whistle, it made him sing:
His heart was mirthful to excess,
But the Rover's mirth was wickedness.

His eye was on the Inchcape float.
Quoth he, "My men, put out the boat
And row me to the Inchcape Rock,
And I'll plague the Abbot of Aberbrothok."

The boat is lowered, the boatmen row,
And to the Inchcape Rock they go;
Sir Ralph bent over from the boat,
And he cut the Bell from the Inchcape float.

Down sank the Bell with a gurgling sound;
The bubbles rose and burst around.
Quoth Sir Ralph, "The next who comes to the Rock
Won't bless the Abbot of Aberbrothok."

Sir Ralph the Rover sailed away;
He scoured the sea for many a day;
And now grown rich with plundered store,
He steers his course for Scotland's shore.

So thick a haze o'erspread the sky,
They cannot see the sun on high:
The wind hath blown a gale all day,
At evening it hath died away.

On the deck the Rover takes his stand;
So dark it is they see no land.
Quoth Sir Ralph, "It will be brighter soon,
For there is the dawn of the rising moon."

"Canst hear," said one, "the broken roar?

For methinks we should be near the shore."
"Now where we are I cannot tell,
But I wish I could hear the Inchcape Bell."

They hear no sound; the swell is strong;
Though the wind hath fallen, they drift along
Till the vessel strikes with a shivering shock:
"O Christ! it is the Inchcape Rock!"

Sir Ralph the Rover tore his hair,
He curst himself in his despair:
The waves rush in on every side,
The ship is sinking beneath the tide.

But, even in his dying fear,
One dreadful sound could the Rover hear,--
A sound as if with the Inchcape Bell
The Devil below was ringing his knell.

I Think Over Again

By Anonymous (Inuit)

I think over again my small adventures,
My fears, those small ones that seemed so big,
For all the vital things I had to get and to reach,
And yet there is only one great thing
The only thing
To live to see the great day that dawns
And the light that fills the world.

Ozymadias of Egypt

By Percy Bysshe Shelley

I met a traveller from an antique land
Who said: "Two vast and trunkless legs of stone
Stand in the desert. Near them on the sand,
Half sunk, a shattered visage lies, whose frown
And wrinkled lip and sneer of cold command
Tell that its sculptor well those passions read
Which yet survive, stamped on these lifeless things,
The hand that mock'd them and the heart that fed;
And on the pedestal these words appear:
'My name is Ozymandias, king of kings:
Look on my works, ye Mighty, and despair!'
Nothing beside remains. Round the decay
Of that colossal wreck, boundless and bare,
The lone and level sands stretch far away;"

Firewarden on Kearsage

By Robert Francis

Rock on the mountain
And on the rock a tower
Sprung like a steel stamen
From a granite flower
And on the tower a man.
Call him a seer.
His slow relentless eyes
Hour after lonely hour
Scan and still scan
Horizons of a hemisphere –
A sky notched compass-wise
Each windy point a peak
Each peak a rock –
Chocorua's curved beak,
Washington, Moosilauke.
Speak: from the west can any shock
Shake of this granite petal?
From the east can any power
Break rock or man or metal?

The Tramps

By Robert William Service

Can you recall, dear comrade, when we tramped God's land together,
And we sang the old, old Earth-song, for our youth was very sweet;
When we drank and fought and lusted, as we mocked at tie and tether,
Along the road to Anywhere, the wide world at our feet --

Along the road to Anywhere, when each day had its story;
When time was yet our vassal, and life's jest was still unstale;
When peace unfathomed filled our hearts as, bathed in amber glory,
Along the road to Anywhere we watched the sunsets pale?

Alas! the road to Anywhere is pitfalled with disaster;
There's hunger, want, and weariness, yet O we loved it so!
As on we tramped exultantly, and no man was our master,
And no man guessed what dreams were ours, as, swinging heel and toe,
We tramped the road to Anywhere, the magic road to Anywhere,
The tragic road to Anywhere, such dear, dim years ago.

Song Of Myself

By Walt Whitman

I celebrate myself, and sing myself,
And what I assume you shall assume,
For every atom belonging to me as good belongs to you.
I loafe and invite my soul,
I lean and loafe at my ease observing a spear of summer grass.
My tongue, every atom of my blood, form'd from this soil, this air,
Born here of parents born here from parents the same, and their parents the same,
I, now thirty-seven years old in perfect health begin,
Hoping to cease not till death.

I harbor for good or bad, I permit to speak at every hazard,
Nature without check with original energy.

Have you reckoned a thousand acres much? have you reckon'd the earth much?
Have you practised so long to learn to read?
Have you felt so proud to get at the meaning of poems?

Stop this day and night with me and you shall possess the origin of all poems,
You shall possess the good of the earth and sun (there are millions of suns left),
You shall no longer take things at second or third hand, nor look through the eyes of the dead, nor feed on the specters in books,
You shall not look through my eyes either, nor take things from me,

You shall listen to all sides and filter them from yourself.

A child said, "_What is the grass?_" fetching it to me with full hands;
How could I answer the child? I do not know what it is any more than he.
I guess it must be the flag of my disposition, out of hopeful green stuff woven.
Or, I guess it is the handkerchief of the Lord,
A scented gift and remembrance designedly dropt,
Bearing the owner's name some way in the corners,
that we may see and remark, and say,
"_Whose?_"

Alone far in the wilds and mountains I hunt,
Wandering amazed at my own lightness and glee,
In the late afternoon choosing a safe spot to pass the night,
Kindling a fire and broiling the fresh-kill'd game,
Falling asleep on the gathered leaves with my dog and gun by my side.
The Yankee clipper is under her sky-sails, she cuts the sparkle and scud,
My eyes settle the land, I bend at her prow or shout joyously from the deck.
The boatman and clam-diggers arose early and stopt for me,
I tucked my trouser-ends in my boots and went and had a good time;
You should have been with us that day round the chowder-kettle.

The runaway slave came to my house and stopt outside,
I heard his motions crackling the twigs of the woodpile,
Through the swung half-door of the kitchen I saw him limpsy and weak,
And went where he sat on a log and led him in and assured him,

And brought water and fill'd a tub for his sweated body and bruis'd feet,
And gave him a room that entered from my own, and gave him some coarse clean clothes,
And remember perfectly well his revolving eyes and his awkwardness,
And remember putting plasters on the galls of his neck and ankles;
He staid with me a week before he was recuperated and passed north,
I had him sit next me at table, my firelock lean'd in the corner.

I am the poet of the woman the same as the man,
And I say it is as great to be a woman as to be a man,
And I say there is nothing greater than the mother of men.

I understand the large hearts of heroes,
The courage of present times and all times,
How the skipper saw the crowded and rudderless wreck of the steamship,
and Death chasing it up and down the storm,
How he knuckled tight and gave not back an inch and was faithful of days and faithful of nights,
And chalked in large letters on a board, "_Be of good cheer, we will not desert you_";
How he followed with them and tack'd with them three days and would not give it up,
How he saved the drifting company at last,
How the lank loose-gown'd women looked when boated from the side of their prepared graves,
How the silent old-faced infants and the lifted sick, and the sharp-lipp'd unshaved men;
All this I swallow, it tastes good, I like it well, it becomes mine,
I am the man, I suffered, I was there.

The disdain and calmness of martyrs,
The mother of old, condemned for a witch, burned with dry wood, her children gazing on,
The hounded slave that flags in the race, leans by the fence blowing,
covered with sweat.
I am the hounded slave, I wince at the bite of the dogs,
Hell and despair are upon me, crack and again crack the marksmen,
I clutch the rails of the fence, my gore dribs, thinn'd with the ooze of my skin,
I fall on the weeds and stones,
The riders spur their unwilling horses, haul close,
Taunt my dizzy ears and beat me violently over the head with whip-stocks.

Old age superbly rising! O welcome, ineffable grace of dying days!

See ever so far, there is limitless space outside of that,
Count ever so much, there is limitless time around that.
My rendezvous is appointed, it is certain,
The Lord will be there and wait till I come on perfect terms.
The great Camerado, the lover true for whom I pine will be there.

And whoever walks a furlong without sympathy walks to his own funeral drest in his shroud.

And to glance with an eye or show a bean in its pod confounds the learning of all times,
And there is no trade or employment but the young man following it may become a hero,
And there is no object so soft but it makes a hub for the wheel'd universe.
And I say to any man or woman, "Let your soul stand cool

and composed before a million universes."

I see something of God each hour of the twenty-four, and each moment then,
In the faces of men and women I see God, and in my own face in the glass,
I find letters from God dropt in the street, and every one is sign'd by God's name,
And I leave them where they are, for I know that wheresoe'er I go,
Others will punctually come forever and ever.

Listener up there! What have you to confide in me?
Look in my face while I snuff the sidle of evening.
(Talk honestly, no one else hears you, and I stay only a minute longer.)
Who has done his day's work? Who will soonest be through with his supper?
Who wishes to walk with me?

I too am not a bit tamed, I too am untranslatable,
I sound my barbaric yawp over the roofs of the world.

I Taste a Liquor Never Brewed

By Emily Dickinson

I taste a liquor never brewed,
From tankards scooped in pearl;
Not all the vats upon the Rhine
Yield such an alcohol!

Inebriate of air am I,
And debauchee of dew,
Reeling, through endless summer days,
From inns of molten blue.

When the landlord turn the drunken bee
Out of the foxglove's door,
When butterflies renounce their drams,
I shall but drink the more!

Till seraphs swing their snowy hats,
And saints to windows run,
To see the little tippler
Leaning against the sun!

The Call Of The Wild

By Robert William Service

Have you gazed on naked grandeur where there's nothing else to gaze on,
Set pieces and drop-curtain scenes galore,
Big mountains heaved to heaven, which the blinding sunsets blazon,
Black canyons where the rapids rip and roar?
Have you swept the visioned valley with the green stream streaking through it,
Searched the Vastness for a something you have lost?
Have you strung your soul to silence? Then for God's sake go and do it;
Hear the challenge, learn the lesson, pay the cost.

Have you wandered in the wilderness, the sagebrush desolation,
The bunch-grass levels where the cattle graze?
Have you whistled bits of rag-time at the end of all creation,
And learned to know the desert's little ways?
Have you camped upon the foothills, have you galloped o'er the ranges,
Have you roamed the arid sun-lands through and through?
Have you chummed up with the mesa? Do you know its moods and changes?
Then listen to the Wild -- it's calling you.

Have you known the Great White Silence, not a snow-gemmed twig aquiver?
(Eternal truths that shame our soothing lies.)

Have you broken trail on snowshoes? mushed your huskies up the river,
Dared the unknown, led the way, and clutched the prize?
Have you marked the map's void spaces, mingled with the mongrel races,
Felt the savage strength of brute in every thew?
And though grim as hell the worst is, can you round it off with curses?
Then hearken to the Wild -- it's wanting you.

Have you suffered, starved and triumphed, groveled down, yet grasped at glory,
Grown bigger in the bigness of the whole?
"Done things" just for the doing, letting babblers tell the story,
Seeing through the nice veneer the naked soul?
Have you seen God in His splendors, heard the text that nature renders?
(You'll never hear it in the family pew.)
The simple things, the true things, the silent men who do things --
Then listen to the Wild -- it's calling you.

They have cradled you in custom, they have primed you with their preaching,
They have soaked you in convention through and through;
They have put you in a showcase; you're a credit to their teaching --
But can't you hear the Wild? -- it's calling you.
Let us probe the silent places, let us seek what luck betide us;
Let us journey to a lonely land I know.
There's a whisper on the night-wind, there's a star agleam to guide us,
And the Wild is calling, calling . . . let us go.

If a Tree Could Wander

By Rumi

Oh, if a tree could wander
and move with foot and wings!
It would not suffer the axe blows
and not the pain of saws!
For would the sun not wander
away in every night ?
How could at ev'ry morning
the world be lighted up?
And if the ocean's water
would not rise to the sky,
How would the plants be quickened
by streams and gentle rain?
The drop that left its homeland,
the sea, and then returned ?
It found an oyster waiting
and grew into a pearl.
Did Yusaf not leave his father,
in grief and tears and despair?
Did he not, by such a journey,
gain kingdom and fortune wide?
Did not the Prophet travel
to far Medina, friend?
And there he found a new kingdom
and ruled a hundred lands.
You lack a foot to travel?
Then journey into yourself!
And like a mine of rubies
receive the sunbeams? print!
Out of yourself? such a journey
will lead you to yourself,
It leads to transformation
of dust into pure gold!

I'm Nobody! Who are you?

By Emily Dickinson

I'm nobody! Who are you?
Are you nobody, too?
Then there's a pair of us - don't tell!
They'd advertise - you know!

How dreary to be somebody!
How public like a frog
To tell one's name the livelong day
To an admiring bog!

Night

By William Blake

The sun descending in the west,
    The evening star does shine;
The birds are silent in their nest.
    And I must seek for mine.
    The moon, like a flower
    In heaven's high bower,
    With silent delight
    Sits and smiles on the night.

Farewell, green fields and happy grove,
    Where flocks have took delight:
Where lambs have nibbled, silent move
    The feet of angels bright;
    Unseen they pour blessing
    And joy without ceasing
    On each bud and blossom,
    And each sleeping bosom.

They look in every thoughtless nest

Where birds are cover'd warm;
They visit caves of every beast,
To keep them all from harm:
If they see any weeping
That should have been sleeping,
They pour sleep on their head,
And sit down by their bed.

When wolves and tigers howl for prey,
They pitying stand and weep,
Seeking to drive their thirst away
And keep them from the sheep.
But, if they rush dreadful,
The angels, most heedful,
Receive each mild spirit,
New worlds to inherit.

And there the lion's ruddy eyes
Shall flow with tears of gold:
And pitying the tender cries,
And walking round the fold:
Saying, 'Wrath, by His meekness,
And, by His health, sickness,
Are driven away
From our immortal day.

'And now beside thee, bleating lamb,
I can lie down and sleep,
Or think on Him who bore thy name,
Graze after thee, and weep.
For, wash'd in life's river,
My bright mane for ever
Shall shine like the gold
As I guard o'er the fold.'

Ode to the West Wind

By Percy Bysshe Shelley

I

O Wild West Wind, thou breath of Autumn's being
    Thou from whose unseen presence the leaves dead
Are driven like ghosts from an enchanter fleeing,

    Yellow, and black, and pale, and hectic red,
Pestilence-stricken multitudes! O thou
    Who chariotest to their dark wintry bed

The winged seeds, where they lie cold and low,
    Each like a corpse within its grave, until
Thine azure sister of the Spring shall blow

    Her clarion o'er the dreaming earth, and fill
(Driving sweet buds like flocks to feed in air)
    With living hues and odours plain and hill;

Wild Spirit, which art moving everywhere;
Destroyer and preserver; hear, O hear!

II

Thou on whose stream, 'mid the steep sky's commotion,
    Loose clouds like earth's decaying leaves are shed,
Shook from the tangled boughs of heaven and ocean,

    Angels of rain and lightning! there are spread
On the blue surface of thine airy surge,
    Like the bright hair uplifted from the head

Of some fierce Maenad, even from the dim verge

Of the horizon to the zenith's height,
The locks of the approaching storm. Thou dirge

Of the dying year, to which this closing night
Will be the dome of a vast sepulchre,
Vaulted with all thy congregated might

Of vapours, from whose solid atmosphere
Black rain, and fire, and hail, will burst: O hear!

III

Thou who didst waken from his summer dreams
The blue Mediterranean, where he lay,
Lull'd by the coil of his crystalline streams,

Beside a pumice isle in Baiae's bay,
And saw in sleep old palaces and towers
Quivering within the wave's intenser day,

All overgrown with azure moss, and flowers
So sweet, the sense faints picturing them! Thou
For whose path the Atlantic's level powers

Cleave themselves into chasms, while far below
The sea-blooms and the oozy woods which wear
The sapless foliage of the ocean, know

Thy voice, and suddenly grow gray with fear,
And tremble and despoil themselves: O hear!

IV

If I were a dead leaf thou mightest bear;
If I were a swift cloud to fly with thee;
A wave to pant beneath thy power, and share

The impulse of thy strength, only less free
Than thou, O uncontrollable! if even
I were as in my boyhood, and could be

The comrade of thy wanderings over heaven,
As then, when to outstrip thy skiey speed
Scarce seem'd a vision--I would ne'er have striven

As thus with thee in prayer in my sore need.
O! lift me as a wave, a leaf, a cloud!
I fall upon the thorns of life! I bleed!

A heavy weight of hours has chain'd and bow'd
One too like thee--tameless, and swift, and proud.

V

Make me thy lyre, even as the forest is:
What if my leaves are falling like its own?
The tumult of thy mighty harmonies

Will take from both a deep autumnal tone,
Sweet though in sadness. Be thou, Spirit fierce,
My spirit! Be thou me, impetuous one!

Drive my dead thoughts over the universe,
Like wither'd leaves, to quicken a new birth;
And, by the incantation of this verse,

Scatter, as from an unextinguish'd hearth
Ashes and sparks, my words among mankind!
Be through my lips to unawaken'd earth

The trumpet of a prophecy! O Wind,
If Winter comes, can Spring be far behind?

Strong Beer

By Robert Graves

"What do you think
The bravest drink
Under the sky?"
"Strong beer," said I.

"There's a place for everything,
Everything, anything,
There's a place for everything
Where it ought to be:
For a chicken, the hen's wing;
For poison, the bee's sting;
For almond-blossom, Spring;
A beerhouse for me."

"There's a prize for every one
Every one, any one,
There's a prize for every one,
Whoever he may be:
Crags for the mountaineer,
Flags for the Fusilier,
For English poets, beer!
Strong beer for me!"

"Tell us, now, how and when
We may find the bravest men?"
"A sure test, an easy test:
Those that drink beer are the best,
Brown beer strongly brewed,
English drink and English food."

Oh, never choose as Gideon chose
By the cold well, but rather those

Who look on beer when it is brown,
Smack their lips and gulp it down.
Leave the lads who tamely drink
With Gideon by the water brink,
But search the benches of the Plough,
The Tun, the Sun, the Spotted Cow,
For jolly rascal lads who pray,
Pewter in hand, at close of day,
"Teach me to live that I may fear
The grave as little as my beer."

Design

By Robert Frost

I found a dimpled spider, fat and white,
On a white heal-all, holding up a moth
Like a white piece of rigid satin cloth—
Assorted characters of death and blight
Mixed ready to begin the morning right,
Like the ingredients of a witches' broth—
A snow-drop spider, a flower like froth,
And dead wings carried like a paper kite.

What had that flower to do with being white,
The wayside blue and innocent heal-all?
What brought the kindred spider to that height,
Then steered the white moth thither in the night?
What but design of darkness to appal?—
If design govern in a thing so small.

A Mile with Me

By Henry Van Dyke

O who will walk a mile with me
Along life's merry way?
A comrade blithe and full of glee,
Who dares to laugh out loud and free,
And let his frolic fancy play,
Like a happy child, through the flowers gay
That fill the field and fringe the way
Where he walks a mile with me.

And who will walk a mile with me
Along life's weary way?
A friend whose heart has eyes to see
The stars shine out o'er the darkening lea,
And the quiet rest at the end o' the day,--
A friend who knows, and dares to say,
The brave, sweet words that cheer the way
Where he walks a mile with me.

With such a comrade, such a friend,
I fain would walk till journeys end,
Through summer sunshine, winter rain,
And then?--Farewell, we shall meet again!

A Little Learning

By Alexander Pope

A little learning is a dangerous thing
Drink deep, or taste not the Pierian spring:
There shallow draughts intoxicate the brain,
And drinking largely sobers us again.
Fired at first sight with what the muse imparts,
In fearless youth we tempt the heights of arts
While from the bounded level of our mind
Short views we take nor see the lengths behind
But more advanced behold with strange surprise,
New distant scenes of endless science rise!"

So pleased at first the towering Alps we try,
Mount o'er the vales, and seem to tread the sky;
The eternal snows appear already past,
And the first clouds and mountains seem the last;
But those attained, we tremble to survey
The growing labours of the lengthened way;
The increasing prospect tires our wandering eyes,
Hill peep o'er hills, and Alps on Alps arise!

Who Walks with Beauty

By David Morton

Who walks with Beauty has no need of fear:
The sun and moon and stars keep pace with him;
Invisible hands restore the ruined year,
And time itself grows beautifully dim.
One hill will keep the footprints of the moon
That came and went a hushed and secret hour;
One star at dusk will yield the lasting boon:
Remembered beauty's white, immortal flower.

Who takes of Beauty wine and daily bread,
Will know no lack when bitter years are lean;
The brimming cup is by, the feast is spread;
The sun and moon and stars his eyes have seen,
Are for his hunger and the thirst he slakes:
The wine of Beauty and the bread he breaks.

Altitude

By Robert Francis

We heard their cries before we saw the crows,
A score of them. But one is not a crow.
The shape is longer, sharper-winged – a hawk.

Coolly he circles round and round, dodging
Their beaks, enduring those he cannot dodge.
But all the while he wheels he also rises.

Slowly, so slowly we can't see him rise.
We see that he is higher than he was.
We hear the anger of the crows come fainter.

At last one crow drops off and then another.
Then five or six are straggling down the sky.
Then only two are left. Then one. Then none.

The hawk is now a fly on a blue wall.
Nothing is near him. He is high enough.
He takes his time, drifting away to west.

Additional Poems that I believe would be of interest to readers.

Corsons Inlet by A.R. Ammons

Still by A.R. Ammons
The Painter by John Ashbery
The More Loving One by W.H. Auden
God's Vagabond by Robert William Service
The Trail of No Return by Robert William Service

Hurt Hawks by Robinson Jeffers

The Perfect High by Sheldon Silverstein

Two Tramps in Mud Time by Robert Frost

For the Union Dead By Robert Lowell

The Peace of Wild Things By Wendell Berry

Nights, By Kevin Hart

Dharma, By Billy Collins

Rain, By Jack Gilbert

Spring and All, By William Carlos Williams

At the Un-National Monument Along the Canadian Border, By William Stafford

A Ritual to Read to Each Other, By William Stafford

Travelling Through the Dark, By William Stafford

Remembering Mountain Men, By William Stafford

The Far Field, By Theodore Roethke

The Meadow Mouse, By Theodore Roethke

Long Live the Weeds, By Theodore Roethke

The Waking, By Theodore Roethke

Learning By Doing, By Howard Nemerov

The Signature of all Things, By Kenneth Rexroth

The Heart of Herakles, By Kenneth Rexroth

Blackberry Eating, By Galway Kinnell

At Great Pond, By Mary Oliver

The Fish, By Mary Oliver

The Armadillo, By Elizabeth Bishop

The Fish, By Elizabeth Bishop

The Girl Who Goes Alone, By Elizabeth Austen

Walking to Oak-Head Pond, and Thinking of the Ponds I Will Visit in the Next Days and Weeks, By Mary Oliver

Wolves in the Zoo, By Howard Nemerov

About the Pacific Crest Trail and the Pacific Crest Trail Association

The Pacific Crest Trail is a 2,650-mile national scenic trail that runs from Mexico to Canada through California, Oregon and Washington. It passes through six out of seven of North America's ecozones including high and low desert, old-growth forest and artic-alpine country

About the Pacific Crest Trail Association

The mission of the Pacific Crest Trail Association is to protect, preserve and promote the Pacific Crest National Scenic Trail as an internationally significant resource for the enjoyment of hikers and equestrians, and for the value that wild and scenic lands provide to all people.

The Pacific Crest Trail Association is a membership organization formed as a nonprofit public benefit corporation and is recognized as a charitable and educational organization under the Internal Revenue Code Section 501(c)3.

They can be reached at www.pcta.org.

www.ingramcontent.com/pod-product-compliance
Lightning Source LLC
LaVergne TN
LVHW090956080826
845145LV00003B/1031

* 9 7 8 0 9 8 3 3 9 8 6 0 8 *